THE KING'S
GERMAN LEGION

From Bexhill to the Battle of Waterloo

THE KING'S GERMAN LEGION

From Bexhill to the Battle of Waterloo

Written and researched by
The Bexhill Hanoverian Study Group

First published in 2003
by The Bexhill Hanoverian Study Group.
© the Bexhill Hanoverian Study Group

A catalogue record for this book is available from
the British Library

Designed by Sara Turner

Printed by Chandlers Printers Ltd,
Saxon Mews,Reginald Road,
Bexhill-on-Sea, East Sussex TN39 3PJ

CONTENTS

ILLUSTRATIONS

INTRODUCTION

The Bexhill Hanoverian Study Group decided (with the approval of the Curator, Mr Julian Porter), to produce a small book to accompany the present permanent King's German Legion exhibition in Bexhill Museum. Extending the whole length of one wall and including table cases, the exhibition is very comprehensive. There are portraits of notable persons, such as King George III, the Duke of Cambridge, Major General Sir Colin Halkett KCB, Lt. General Charles Count von Alten, KCB, Colonel Baron Christian von Ompteda, Major George Baring and so on, not forgetting the principal characters, Wellington and Napoleon.

Four figures, each about two foot high, are mounted on the display board; in one pair is an Officer of a K.G.L. Cavalry Regiment together with an Officer of the K.G.L. 2nd Light Battalion, and in the other a Private of a K.G.L. Line Battalion armed with a Brown Bess Musket and a Rifleman of a K.G.L. Light Battalion with a Baker Rifle.

At each end of the exhibition is a free-standing and life-size K.G.L. figure, one representing a Sergeant of the Sharpshooters, 2nd Light Battalion and the other a Sergeant of the Sharpshooters Light Company, 3rd Line Battalion. A reproduction K.G.L. Line Battalion jacket, together with a framed photograph of the German K.G.L. Re-enactment Group taken at La Haye Sainte, is displayed in one table case and, in another, are some models of 1½ inch K.G.L. soldiers depicting Hussars, Dragoons, Horse and Foot Artillery complete with guns, and K.G.L. Light Infantry in action.

The first K.G.L. exhibition in 1990 was a temporary one opened by the late Lady Longford. It was entitled "From Bexhill to the Battle of Waterloo – The King's German Legion" (175th Anniversary of the Battle). In 1991, a permanent display was launched by Dr. Peter Boyden of the National Army Museum.

Some of the images in this book may be of poor quality because they are archive material.

The Bexhill Hanoverian Study Group is responsible for the above-mentioned K.G.L. exhibition.

UNIFORMS OF THE KING'S GERMAN LEGION

1st Dragoons (1803)

2nd Dragoons (1812)

1st Light Infantry

Skirmishers

Artillery

Private of Foot Artillery

2nd Hussars

3rd Hussars

Skirmishers

Line Battalions

2nd Light Infantry

Line Battalions

THE KING'S GERMAN LEGION

Because of the threat posed by the French Revolution in 1789, military encampments were established along the South Coast of England. Many became permanent barracks, including those at Bexhill which dated from 1798.

Additional quarters were set up at Bexhill when soldiers were needed to help build the Martello towers. The village population was around 2,000 and there were about a hundred houses. Imagine the impact on the place in 1804, when five or six thousand Hanoverian troops arrived. There were four battalions of them – Bexhill had been chosen as an infantry depot!

The origins of the King's German Legion lay in defeat. The Elector of Hanover also happened to be George III of England. When his army was beaten by the French, he appointed the troops as a separate force within the British Army.

The barracks* stretched for twenty-five acres between Belle Hill, Chantry Lane and what is now London Road, with the parade ground running east to west. It was built on the north side of the hill, so that any Frenchmen lurking out at sea would not spot it. Later, the camp extended onto Bexhill Down, with outposts at Little Common. Major General Sir Arthur Wellesley (later the Duke of Wellington) was in command of the main brigade at Hastings. He would have inspected the troops at the parade grounds which lay behind Barrack Hall, Bexhill Old Town.

The soldiers of the King's German Legion, when at Bexhill, worshipped at St. Peter's Church, Old Town and their harmonious singing soon endeared them to the local inhabitants. These soldiers too took great care of their horses which, of course, needed replacement and reshoeing, thereby creating employment for the tradesmen of Bexhill.

St. Peter's Church

---

* Bexhill had no housing facilities for more than a handful of officers. The troops therefore first of all lived in tents, then in simple huts with straw roofs which were very unsatisfactory. Violent storms in the autumn of 1804 brought flooding and misery to the camp.

Obviously, the troops needed provisions and Pocock's Butcher Shop, Old Town (now unfortunately closed) provided the King's German Legion with meat. The Legion would have frequented the local public houses such as "The Bell Inn", "The Black Horse" (later renamed "The Queen's Head"★), "The Gun"★★ and "The New Inn" at Sidley, where the K.G.L. set up a bowling alley.

Duke of Cambridge

No doubt you are wondering how this all began. In 1803 a French Army led by General Mortier invaded and occupied the Electorate of Hanover, the domain of Britain's George III. The King's seventh son, Adolphus Frederick, Duke of Cambridge, fulfilling the role of Viceroy, was anxious to lead the ill-prepared Hanoverian Army against the French, but the Electorate's leading politicians, currying favour with the invaders, frustrated his plans. Thoroughly disgusted, the Duke sailed home with the Hanoverian aides-de-camp.

Officers, including Baron Christian von Ompteda, responded enthusiastically but other ranks were slow in coming forward, fearing they might be sent to distant and unhealthy colonies. However, a second and more promising royal proclamation resulted in a flood of volunteers. The decree authorised the establishing in the British Army of a corps to be known as the King's German Legion, with the Duke of Cambridge as its Colonel-in-Chief.

By the autumn of 1803, there was a steady flow of officers and other ranks of the former Hanoverian Army passing through the port of Husum in Schleswig Holstein en route to Heligoland. From there British Naval Transports conveyed them to Portsmouth. In nearby Lymington the recruits were posted to Cavalry, Artillery and Infantry Regiments. An Engineer unit of officers was also established.

Christian von Ompteda

* "The Queen's Head" (demolished when King Offa Way was constructed): The landlord of this pub made hessian boots for the King's German Legion.
** "The Gun": Later St. Francis School was built on the West Down Road site and subsequently modern dwellings.
Note: "The Bell Inn" in Bexhill Old Town and "The New Inn" in Sidley still exist.

In a matter of months the K.G.L. consisted of 2 Regiments of Cavalry, 2 Light Battalions, 4 Line Battalions, 2 Horse Batteries of Artillery, 3 Foot Batteries of Artillery and a unit of Engineers. By 1806, 7,876 officers and other ranks were serving. Within a year the Legion had doubled its size. By 1816 more than 25,000 men had served with the K.G.L. over a period of thirteen years, so heavy were the casualties suffered by the Corps.

Old Bexhill Barracks in lower Belle Hill area by Francis Grose.

The main Cavalry Depot was established at Radipole Barracks in Weymouth. Subsidiary depots were centred in Ipswich, Guildford and Canterbury. The main Infantry Depot and Artillery Depot were sited in 1804 in the Barracks at Bexhill. These barracks were founded in 1798. Here there seems to have been established a permanent K.G.L. Garrison Battalion which in 1813 was incorporated into a Veteran Battalion. There were 25 acres of Infantry Barracks on the North West slopes of the hill, shielded from the sea and the beaches. At the top of the Down were about 15 acres of Cavalry and Artillery Barracks.

The Infantry Barracks site included a Military Cemetery at Barrack Road where hundreds of military personnel and dependants were buried over the years, including at least 152 members of the K.G.L. Later the cemetery was used as an extension of St. Peter's Churchyard.

In 1994 the Bexhill Hanoverian Study Group, together with the Bexhill Old Town Preservation Society, erected a plaque in the Memorial Gardens, Barrack Road, Bexhill, in memory of those people. This was a very moving ceremony with the late Lady Longford, the Study Group's patron, unveiling the plaque. A Re-enactment Group was in attendance and, upon the unveiling, sounded the 'Last Post' and fired a volley of shots over the graves.

No. 4 Company 2nd Light Battalion
K.G.L., and the XV Hussars
Re-enactment Groups, in attendance
(on 23rd April 1994) at the unveiling
of the plaque in Memorial Gardens,
Bexhill, dedicated to several hundred
soldiers of the British Army, including
over 150 personnel of King George
III's King's German Legion.

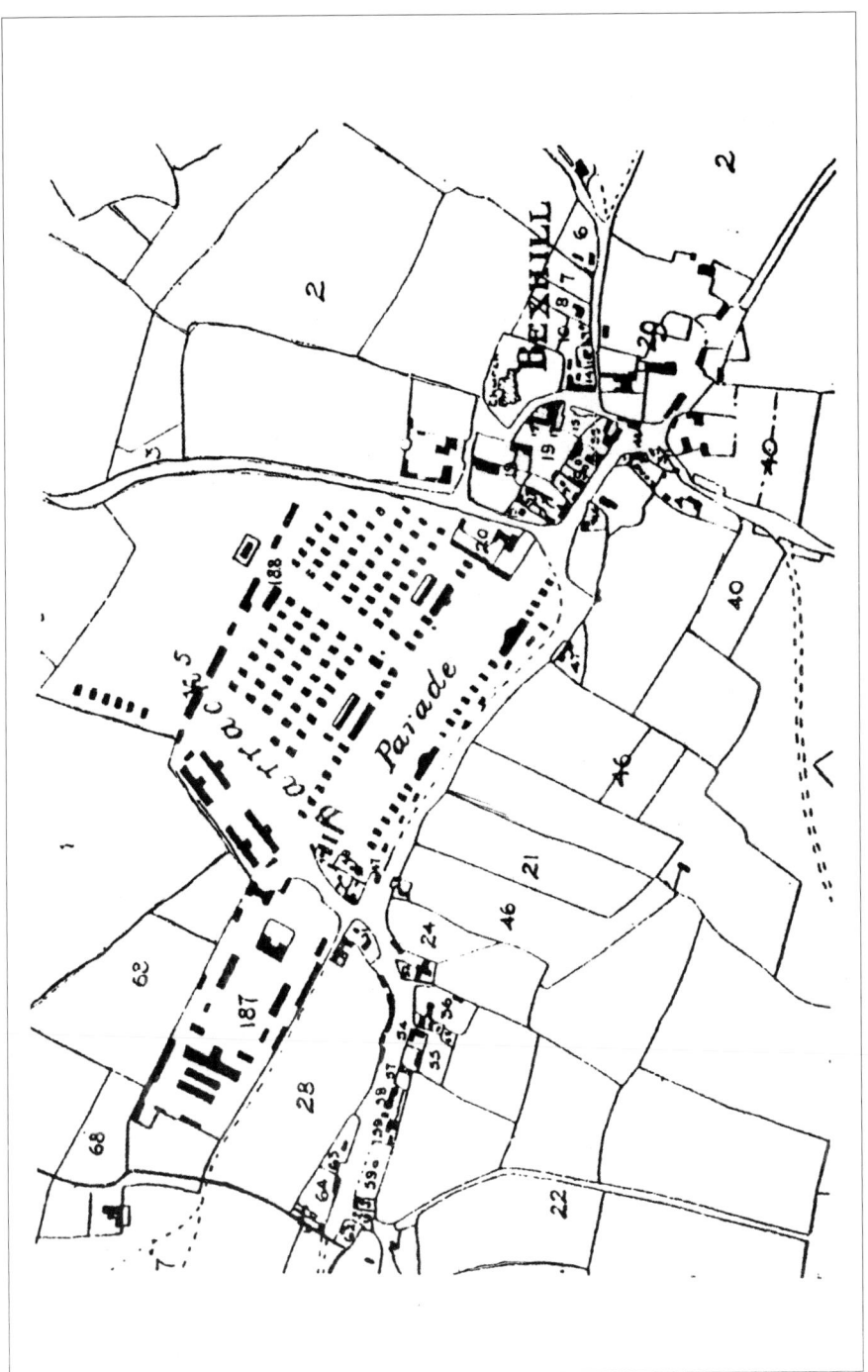

Part of Bexhill Manor map during the Napoleonic Wars, showing the barracks of the King's German Legion.

Light Bns. King's German Legion.

1. *Sergeant, Sharpshooters, 2nd Light Bn., K.G.L., 1815*

2. *Officer, 2nd Light Bn., K.G.L., 1815*

3. *Private, 1st Light Bn., K.G.L., 1815*

Bexhill Village from north east, 1794. (Lane in foreground is Hastings Road.)

A Martello tower

Bexhill Barracks ranked among the largest in the country according to Professor John Breihan of Loyola College, Baltimore, U.S.A., who visited the site in 1989 whilst researching the subject of Barracks in Britain. Bexhill Barracks had great strategic importance having easy access to about fifteen miles of beach between Hastings and Eastbourne, on which stood a line of Martello towers. British Army engineers had alerted the Government that this was an ideal area for Napoleon to land the fleet of flat bottomed boats which he had massed at Boulogne, almost opposite, across the English Channel.

Fortunately Nelson's victory at the Battle of Trafalgar in 1805 frustrated Napoleon's invasion plans. As a result, the King's German Legion, which had been especially chosen to play a leading part in repelling the French, began eleven years of distinguished active service in other theatres of the war. These included North Germany, 1804; the Baltic area, 1807; the Mediterranean and Sicily, 1808–1811; the Peninsula and Southern France, 1808–1814; Walcheren, 1809; Italy, 1814; North Germany, 1813–1814; Malta and Sicily, 1812–1816 and finally at Waterloo in 1815 where they held key positions in the centre of the line, alongside the elite of the British Army.

The K.G.L. gained numerous Battle Honours, including Gibraltar, the Pensinula and Waterloo, all remembered in North-West Germany to this day.

In the small town of Goslar, about forty miles south-east of Hanover, was garrisoned a Jäger Battalion, formerly of the Royal Guard, which is directly descended from the 1st and 2nd Light Battalions of the King's German Legion.

The regimental war memorial in the town particularly mentions their period of service with the K.G.L. These Light Battalions were closely involved with Bexhill, even helping with the initial excavation of the wrecked "Amsterdam" at Bulverhythe. There were local marriages, births and deaths too, all recorded in St. Peter's Church Register.

But what of our story? K.G.L. regiments of all arms finally advanced with Wellington's Army into southern France in 1814 and shared in the initial victory over Napoleon. Likewise, other K.G.L. units were involved in N.W. Europe and the Mediterranean countries. This brings us back to where we began in the summer of 1814.

While K.G.L. Cavalry made their way across France to the Low Countries, the K.G.L. Infantry were re-mustered here at Bexhill. Their numbers exceeded 5,000. Little wonder Bexhill was agog with excitement!

Napoleon's escape from Elba changed everything. Wellington was thankful to be able to recall his Peninsula veterans of the K.G.L. because many seasoned British regiments had been posted to the Colonies. Once again these elite Hanoverians stood shoulder to shoulder with their British comrades in the centre of the Allied Line at Waterloo.

The Farmhouse, La Haye Sainte

The 2nd Light Battalion, led by Major George Baring, with reinforcements from the 1st Light Battalion, were out in front of the line holding as a strong point the farm, La Haye Sainte. In a similar manner, British Guards with K.G.L. pioneers were defending Hougoumont Farm on the right. At La Haye Sainte, Major George Baring and some 400 men frustrated Napoleon's efforts to break through by pouring fire into their flanks. He was to swear later, on St. Helena, that the

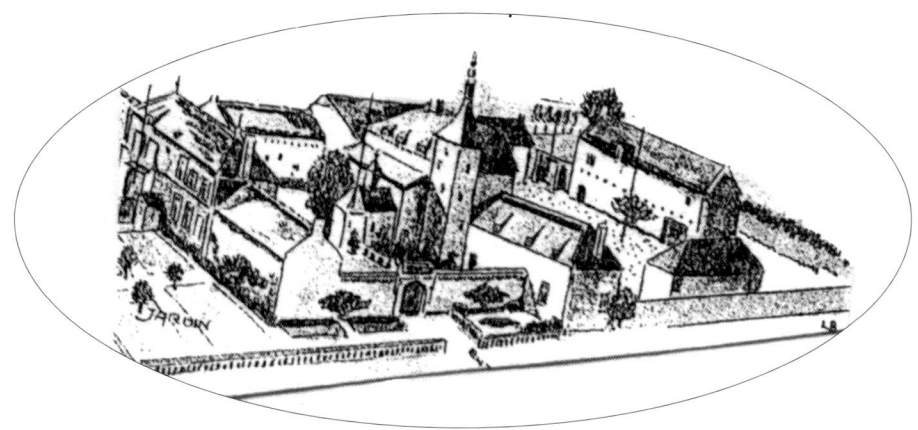

Hougoumont

stubborn resistance met at La Haye Sainte had cost him the battle. The K.G.L. men fought heroically until late afternoon when they ran out of ammunition for their Baker Rifles.

Desperately, they resisted the onslaughts of the French with rifle butts and bayonets. Finally they were ordered to withdraw to the Allied line. Barely forty, including an injured Major Baring, survived. In the confusion George Baring became separated from his men who were searching for ammunition. Finding a mount Major Baring fell in with the K.G.L. Hussars.

Meanwhile the British 3rd Division commanded by General Sir Charles von Alten of the K.G.L., the only German General ever to command a British Division, was very heavily engaged with the enemy. Alten's 2nd Brigade led by Colonel Christian von Ompteda of the K.G.L. was ordered, very unwisely, by the 1st Corps Commander, the Prince of Orange, to advance in line. This brought disaster. Initially the cheering men of Ompteda's 5th Battalion drove back the enemy infantry but French Cavalry nearby turned on them and cut them down. Colonel Ompteda, out in front, was shot in the throat and killed. By his side fell Lieutenant Edmund Wheatley who, in 1812, had joined the Legion at Bexhill. Luckily he was only stunned and later taken prisoner. After some rough handling he managed to escape during the French retreat.

Major Baring

After Napoleon's defeat at Waterloo in 1815, the King's German Legion returned to Hanover, taking with it not a few Bexhill brides. Much of the huge camp was then demolished.

KGL 1st Light Battalion 1808

Additional notes regarding notable persons in the King's German Legion Exhibition at Bexhill Museum

Napoleon Bonaparte

Napoleon, who was born in Corsica in 1769, began his military career as a junior artillery officer. In the aftermath of the French Revolution he survived several potentially disastrous situations. In 1795 his swift suppression of a Parisian insurrection, which threatened to overturn the government, resulted in his being appointed Commander of the Army of the Interior. This was the beginning of great things and by 1804 Napoleon had crowned himself Emperor.

His downfall began with his ambitious invasion of Russia in 1812; it was settled by his defeat at Leipzig in 1813 and Wellington's successful conclusion of the Peninsular War in 1814. By April of that year he was en route to the Mediterranean island of Elba.

Napoleon's audacious escape in March 1815 and incredible re-organisation of the French Army was, however, eclipsed by the cool courage of the Allied army at Waterloo, the superb strategy of Wellington and the loyalty of the Prussian Commander-in-Chief, Field Marshal von Blücher. These qualities despatched Napoleon unceremoniously to the South Atlantic and St. Helena, in the care of His Majesty's Navy, which throughout his campaigns had frustrated his ambitions.

The Duke of Wellington

Arthur Wellesley, the first Duke of Wellington, had one thing in common with his arch enemy – he too was born in 1769. Born in Ireland, the son of an Anglo–Irish nobleman, he was educated at Eton and at a French Military Academy. Then followed service in both the British Army and politics. The military experience gained in India and the Peninsular War, plus his own brand of cool, calculating genius, enabled him to out-manoeuvre Napoleon and, with Blücher's help, destroy the French Army at Waterloo.

He thought highly of the King's German Legion which, together with many newly raised Hanoverian regiments, formed almost half of the British contingent. He entrusted to the K.G.L. vital positions in the centre of the action, including the defence of La Haye Sainte Farm.

The Duke of Cambridge

Adolphus Frederick was the seventh son of George III. He attended the University of Göttingen in the Electorate of Hanover with two of his brothers. Afterwards he followed a life-long career in both the Hanoverian and British Armies.

In 1801 he was created Duke of Cambridge. On the formation of the King's German Legion in 1803, George III appointed the Duke of Cambridge Colonel-in-Chief. His adjutant-general was Colonel Frederick von der Decken.

The Office of the King's German Legion was in Chelsea, the main Cavalry Depot at Weymouth and the main Infantry Depot at Bexhill.

Unlike his brothers, the Duke was never involved in scandal. He married Princess Augusta of Hesse-Cassell in 1818 and they had a son, George, and two daughters. Prince George, born in March 1819, was heir presumptive, until the birth of Princess Victoria in May 1819.

Colonel Baron Christian von Ompteda

Christian von Ompteda, a member of a Hanoverian noble family, began a distinguished military career in 1777 as a member of the Royal Corps of Pages in Hanover. In 1781, aged sixteen, he was appointed as Ensign in the Hanoverian Foot Guards. He was a very loyal and efficient officer and on intimate terms with members of the Royal Family.

He was among the first to offer his services to the Crown after the fall of the Electorate. With the personal approval of the Duke of Cambridge he was appointed commanding officer of the 1st Line Battalion of the K.G.L.

During the winter of 1804 at Bexhill, he became ill and left the barracks to be billeted at Woodgate Farm in Gunters Lane, the home at that time of John Lansdell and family. He was very impressed with the kindness shown to him. (Memoirs of Ompteda).

He saw much active service in Spain and elsewhere but serious ill-health interfered with his career. At Waterloo Colonel von Ompteda commanded the 2nd K.G.L. Infantry Brigade in General von Alten's 3rd Division. Ompteda was killed at La Haye Sainte.

Lieutenant General Charles Count von Alten K.C.B.

General von Alten is the only German officer ever to have commanded a British Army Division. He served throughout the Napoleonic wars and, as an infantry officer, he would have been a frequent visitor to the Depot at Bexhill. While serving at Waterloo in the centre of the Anglo-Allied Line, as the Commanding Officer of the British 3rd Division, he was severely wounded.

After Waterloo he played an important part in the re-establishing of the Hanoverian Army.

Major George Baring *(See page 19)*

Major Baring evidently served with the K.G.L. from the early years. He commanded the 2nd Light Battalion at Waterloo and showed exemplary leadership in the defence of the farm La Haye Sainte. He was honoured and promoted as Major-General Baron von Baring.

Major General Sir Colin Halkett KCB

Colin Halkett, a young Scottish officer, was granted authority in 1803 to raise a battalion of Hanoverian Infantry after the State of Hanover fell to the French.

In the same year he joined forces with Colonel von Decken and under the supreme command of George III's seventh son Adolphus, Duke of Cambridge, who was very popular with the Hanoverians, helped to form the King's German Legion. General Colin Halkett commanded the 5th British Brigade in Gen. Sir Charles Alten's 3rd British Division at Waterloo.

Colonel Hugh Halkett

Hugh Halkett was the younger brother of Major General Sir Colin Halkett. He served, like his brother, from the early days of the K.G.L. He was a frequent visitor to Bexhill Barracks and eventually became the Commanding Officer of the 7th Line Battalion. At Waterloo Hugh Halkett was seconded from the K.G.L. to the command of the newly formed 3rd Hanoverian Brigade in Lieutenant-General Sir Henry Clinton's Second Division.

In the closing and chaotic phase of the battle, while advancing at Hougoumont, Colonel Halkett captured single handed the French General Cambronne.

Edmund Wheatley

Edmund Wheatley of Hammersmith, London was gazetted Ensign in the K.G.L. in November 1812.

He reported to the Infantry Depot at Bexhill and was subsequently posted to the 5th Line Battalion of the K.G.L., which, at that time, was fighting in the Spanish Peninsula. He made a close friend of another British Officer in the regiment named Henry Llewellyn, whose portrait he sketched and included in his remarkable diary.

As Lieutenant Wheatley, he served under Colonel Ompteda at Waterloo and took part in that ill-fated charge which cost the Colonel his life. Wheatley was rendered unconscious by his Colonel's side and was held prisoner by the French during their retreat. In the confusion that followed Edmund Wheatley managed to escape.

Wheatley's dairy is one of the few written on active service. It was dedicated to his sweetheart, Eliza Brookes, whose family disapproved of him. He evidently overcame their opposition, perhaps by his courage and bravery, and married Eliza in February 1820 at St. Andrew-by-the-Wardrobe Church (Queen Victoria Street) in London. They were blessed with three daughters.

The First King's German Legion Exhibition in Bexhill Museum (1990)

This drawing was produced by a nine-year-old boy when visiting Bexhill Museum. The King's German Legion Exhibition is of great interest to children, particularly the two free-standing life-sized K.G.L. figures, one representing a Sergeant of the Sharpshooters 2nd Light Battalion and the other a Sergeant of the Sharpshooters Light Company, 3rd Line Battalion, both of which the youngsters love to draw.

Also, the Curator, Mr Julian Porter, welcomes parties of local High School students to the Museum, where he gives most interesting talks regarding the history of the K.G.L. and the Battle of Waterloo. Recently, the History Department of the High School, as part of their GCSE course, studied the history of Bexhill Barracks and the K.G.L., the project forming part of their assessment.

An extract from Memoirs of
Christian Frederick William Baron Ompteda

The Memoirs of Christian Frederick William Baron Ompteda (Colonel in the King's German Legion) were edited by his grand-nephew Baron Louis von Ompteda, and published in Germany. An English translation, under the title of "A Hanoverian–English Officer A Hundred Years Ago. Memoirs of Baron Ompteda" by John Hill, M.A., was published by H. Grevel & Co., in 1892.

Christian Frederick William Baron Ompteda was born on November 26th 1765. In 1777 (then barely 12) he entered the Royal Corps of Pages at Hanover and in that capacity began his military career. In 1781 (at 16) he received appointment as Ensign (Fahndrich) in the Foot Guards.

"The French had ... at the close of the year 1792, advanced on Holland. George III determined, therefore, to place an English army there and, to add to this, an 'Auxiliary Corps' of from 12,000 to 13,000 men of his Hanoverian troops in English pay. The contingent was included in this ... and in May 1793 Christian stood, with his regiment, in the Netherlands.

"He was of unusual height, with a slender, but symmetrically proportioned build. In the army and at home he went by the name of 'The long gentleman'. ... A good miniature of the date 1793 shows us Christian as a young man of 27 years. A remarkably high and broad forehead, half-long blond hair combed backward and slightly powdered. Under finely curved brows, two mighty big blue eyes, earnest and deep, with an unmistakable tinge of melancholy. The nose curved with a fine bridge, thin silent shut lips, and the beardless fashion of the period ...

"His appearance was very attractive ... his character was noble and morally pure, sustained by a strict sense of honour. His behaviour to others betokened a sympathetic good will, and his treatment of his brothers and relations always testifies the greatest love, devotion and care for their best interests ... he has fully mastered the English, French and Italian languages and read the Latin writers fluently ... As a handsome, entertaining and accomplished man – he played the violin very well – he has the most favourable reception in society. ..."

Ompteda was wounded in the leg at Mount Cassel on September 5th, 1793.

He was killed at Waterloo on June 18th 1815, under circumstances in which he showed great bravery and earned special mention in the Duke of Wellington's first report of the Battle.

**Extracts from: A Hanoverian–English Officer A Hundred Years Ago.
Memoirs of Baron Ompteda.
Translated by John Hill. London. H. Grevel & Co. 1892.**

1804: This year was devoted to the completion and training of the Legion. The
1st Line Battalion was stationed close to Portsmouth until the summer, and later
on, from August at Bexhill, near Hastings. This was because the time had arrived
when England seriously expected an attempt at invasion by Buonaparte, and was
preparing every force on land and water to resist it. Wherefore a quantity of
troops of the most varied description was collected on that part of the coast of
the Channel, and military movements of unusual activity were taking place. At the
same time, a satisfactory spirit of comradeship was developing, as the higher
English officers quickly and readily recognised the efficiency and capability of the
immigrated (Hanoverians) and looked on their officers as "gentlemen". Even the
residents in the large country seats in the neighbourhood displayed various
symptoms of sociability to them.

It is a remarkable proof of the isolation of England at that time, as well as
Christian's absorption in his revived profession that he wrote only three letters to
his brother in Berlin in all the year. The safest means was always employed for the
transmission of these. As the French frequently intercepted couriers, it was a
matter of anxiety lest those addressed in the Fatherland should be compromised.

Diary. "*August 6th (1804):* Midday, first visit to the village of Bexhill, whither the
1st L.B. had been transferred. The people at this place and about the
neighbourhood, generally seem to look on us much as we do on Cossacks." (Later
on.) "The gentry round called at the camp. They seem to be beginning to discover
that we are not quite outlandish bears."
"*August 13th:* General Don has taken command of us. He issued a flattering
inauguratory order: 'Excellent officers and gallant men, the composition of the
Legion'. I look on this in the light of a bill drawn on us. Dishonour it, and you
will be bankrupt! Later on he said, verbally 'Now I have seen the state of the
King's German Legion, I wish Buonaparte would come over tomorrow'."
"*October 11th:* Violent storm and pouring rain last night and all day today. The
ground where our camp is, bad any way, is now a morass and the present quarters
are bad for the men. Beginning to build huts."
"*October 29th:* The camp a swamp. Confined to my tent."
"*November 5th:* Continued cold and bad weather. Being unwell, find my field-bed
only a partial shelter. Ceaseless din of all kinds of bad music, meaningless shoutings

and clamour. All this is trying to the patience, and leads to sullen stupefaction. This is the anniversary of the Gunpowder Plot and Guy Fawkes consequently burnt with huzzas and jubilation in several bonfires in my proximity."

"*November 13th:* Left camp today; of all the uncomfortable ones I have known, the worst ... the wet and stuffiness of my tent delayed my recovery and I as obliged, unwilling though I was not to share our common hardships, to obey the warnings of reason and necessity. A neighbouring farm (Woodgate) became my refuge. Contrast between the dwellings of the English and German peasantry. Comfort, even luxury, but of the most rational description. Agreeable impression of the innocent mirth of the family after the wild disturbances of the camp. Fresh experience.

"*November 15th:* Morning call on the people of the house. Met Miss Mary Lansdell, the daughter of my host. Neatness of costume of this girl, who is, after all, neither more or less than a fairly well-to-do peasant. Her politeness, in showing me over the house. Elegant appointments, mahogany chairs with horsehair seats, carpet, mirror, a fine fireplace and exotics in the room I occupy. Precautions that the labourers and maids when coming home from dirty work should not soil the house. Cleanliness of these lower orders. No shouting and noise. Four men and two boys do their work as quietly and cleverly as if they were skilled artisans plying a handicraft. No ill-tempered horses to be seen."

"*November 16th:* Pure dry air and the return of natural warmth have in these few days brought about great progress in my convalescence. One of the most beneficent advantages of this place is its quiet, which I have been deprived of for a whole year in the incessant din of barrack and camp life."

"*November 20th:* The weather being pleasant, I went to visit the camp. The ground has got worse. Had a look at the huts intended for the use of the battalion; they are still a long way from being ready. Those already inhabited damp, natural consequences of using green wood."

(The general state of health had suffered so much that all the officers who wished to find other lodgings than the huts, were given a special allowance to find quarters with.)

"*November 26th:* Reported myself again for duty. I expected to occupy my hut, but owing to the wet, one of the turf-sod walls had subsided, and had to be rebuilt."

"*December 1st:* Left Woodgate Farm and have gone into my hut. The lime on the walls still very damp and the air uncommonly unwholesome."

"*December 20th:* Increasing severe cold with rough weather. Our draughty huts afford very insufficient shelter against such a climate."

These conditions had a deteriorating effect on the smart appearance of the men. We learn from the battalion journal later on that Lieutenant-Colonel Ompteda issued an order that "no beards were to be worn any more, and that the pioneers and drummers were to shave theirs off". At that time the troops still wore the pigtail, which was only dropped in 1808.

On the last day of the year, Christian Ompteda became Lieutenant-Colonel and Commander of the battalion. As his seniority was not yet quite sufficient, the Duke of Cambridge became nominal colonel of the battalion, in order to ensure Ompteda against the intrusion of any senior staff officer from among those newly come over in the meantime. That was a mark of distinction applying to the old Foot Guards as well as to their present leader.

1805

The year 1805 was also in greater part spent in training the troops, and in heightened suspense as to when and how the storm threatening from Boulogne would discharge itself. The ever-regular clock of duty varied so little, that whole weeks are skipped in the diary for want of anything to write down; and what did happen was mostly unpleasant.

"On March 4th, the mess-house, only just finished, was handed over for the use of the 1st Line Battalion. I utilised this as a becoming opportunity to invite General Don, the English officers of the Prince of Wales' regiment, as well as the officers of the staffs of our battalions which are here, to dine at our mess. The festivities proceeded tolerably well till late in the evening, when, through a careless accident, a boiling tea-kettle got spilt over my hands and legs. A bad scalding, much pain, and confinement for more than four weeks to my quarters, were the consequences. To cheer me, anxiously expected letters arrived, eleven being in arrear, all coming from Husum by the same mail."

On March 20th we hear of "continued pain from my wounds, and incapacity to make any movement worth speaking of." This went on nearly the same till April 4th. The person to blame for this "careless accident" is most generously left unnamed. Another accident, this time harmless, took place on April 11th.
"Out for a walk today I was almost grazed by a musket-ball which was discharged by an Englishman who was letting off a firearm for the first time in his life. On my remonstrating, he assured me that it should not occur again."
Later on, Christian had a fall with his horse and received a contusion of the head, which again confined him to his quarters.

Extract from the Sussex Advertiser 22nd July 1822, page 1
(Supplied by Mr Peter Cole)

"Barrack Materials for SALE on the Barrack Ground at BEXHILL, Sussex.

Typical 18/19 century Army Barracks building
This was the Officers Mess Maidstone until 1900s

A large Quantity of good MATERIALS consisting of Oak and Fir Timbers in Scantlings, Weather Boarding, ¾ inch and ½ inch Boards, Sashes and Frames, Window Shutters, Doors and Door Cases, Dressers, Closet Fronts and Shelves, Stone Hearths, Jambs and Mantles, Window Sills and a variety of other useful Articles.

Also several ENTIRE BUILDINGS, such as a substantial well-framed Timber Building, 130 feet 3 inches long by 21 feet 4 inches wide with two timber and boarded floors throughout, 7 feet 9 inches between lower floor and ceiling.

One other Timber Building, with two floors as above, 74 feet 4 inches long by 29 feet 3 inches wide, and 9 feet 1 inch between lower floor and ceiling.

Three Timber Buildings 25 feet 4 inches long each by 13 fcet wide, height, including sill and plate, 7 foot 2 inches.

One ditto 34 feet 3 inches long by 21 feet wide; height including sill and plate 10 feet 10 inches;
One ditto with folding doors, 14 feet 6 inches front by 16 feet 11 inches; height, including sill and plate 10 feet. The above are all covered with plain tiles. Several other Brick and Timber Buildings and a great quantity of good Bricks and Tiles.

Apply to THOMAS CATLEY, on the Ground, every Thursday, Friday and Saturday. (If by letter, post paid.)

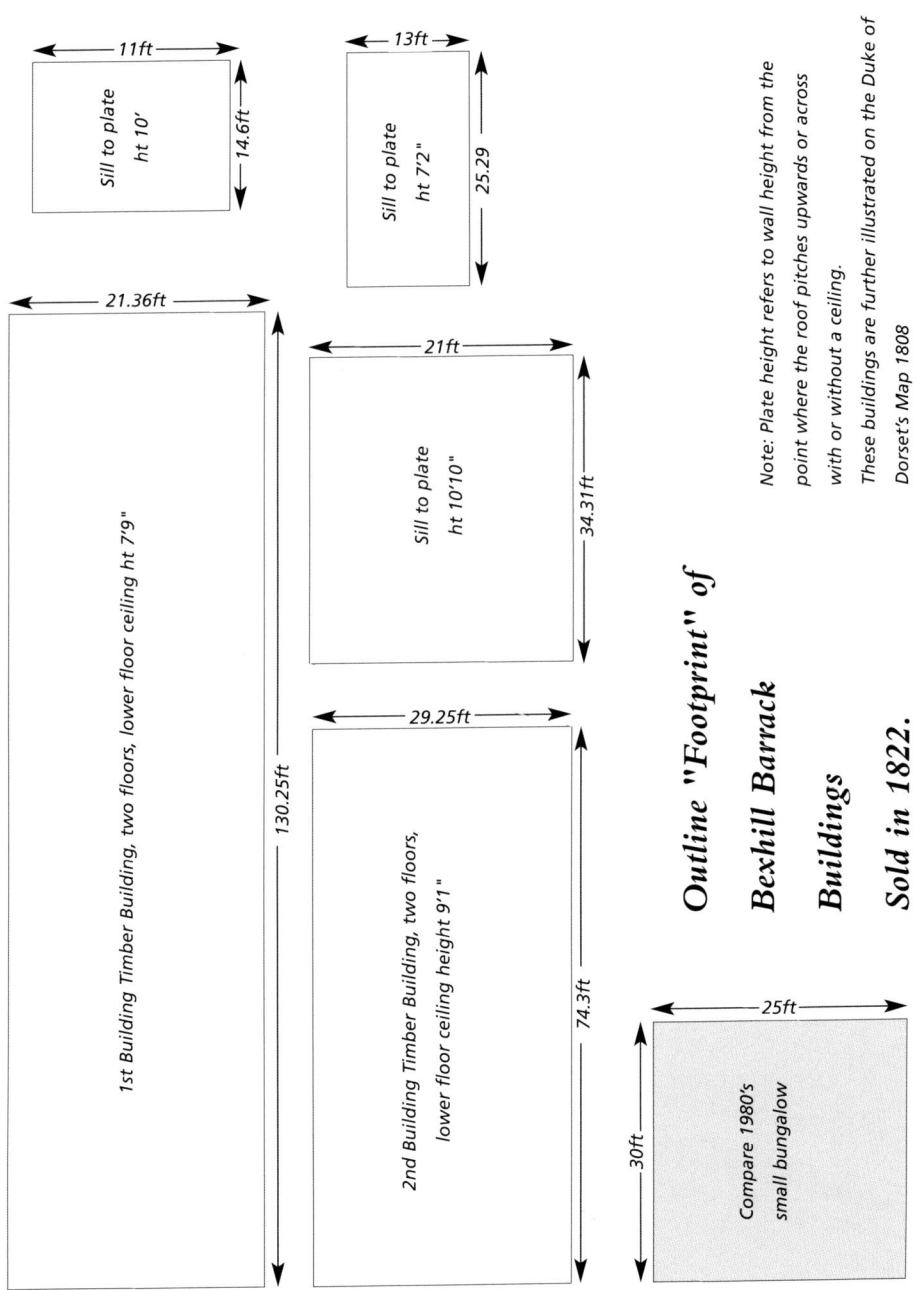

Outline "Footprint" of Bexhill Barrack Buildings Sold in 1822.

Sill to plate ht 10'
11ft
14.6ft

Sill to plate ht 7'2"
13ft
25.29

Note: Plate height refers to wall height from the point where the roof pitches upwards or across with or without a ceiling.

These buildings are further illustrated on the Duke of Dorset's Map 1808

1st Building Timber Building, two floors, lower floor ceiling ht 7'9"
21.36ft
130.25ft

Sill to plate ht 10'10"
21ft
34.31ft

2nd Building Timber Building, two floors, lower floor ceiling height 9'1"
29.25ft
74.3ft

Compare 1980's small bungalow
25ft
30ft

This 'Footprint' is Peter Cole's interpretation of the details of Bexhill Barracks given in the extract of the Sussex Advertiser – it gives some concept of how it relates to a modern bungalow in floor area.

Some interesting buildings in Bexhill Old Town

About the Buildings

A. BARRACK HALL. This building in Bexhill Town adjoins the parade ground of the King's German Legion. The parade ground is now partially used as allotments and various pieces of clay pipes and the occasional button have been found there. During a recently carried out re-location of the allotments, a musket ball was found in the area of the parade ground.

B. WOODGATE FARM. This is where Colonel Christian von Ompteda convalesced after an illness; he was believed to have suffered what we would today call a nervous breakdown. The farm house remains but there has been much building work done and the premises are now used as a school.

C. HANOVER HOUSE. Believed to have been initially owned by a German officer but research has so far been unable to establish who this might be.

D. GODDARD HOUSE. Some officers provided their own accommodation and it is quite possible that the commanding officer of the King's German Legion, Major General Sir Charles Alten, lived there.

E. THE BELL INN. This stands nearby St. Peter's Church, Bexhill by the old Hastings Road and, at its rear, there is a short row of houses believed to have been erected for the influx of the King's German Legion. The Bell Inn would have been frequented by the troops of the K.G.L.

F. THE HOUSE OF THOMAS PUMPHREY. The main duty of the Legion would have been to patrol and observe this Sussex shoreline against any attempt at invasion by the French but they would also have been employed in other duties. Smuggling was a popular pastime and a Customs Officer, Thomas Pumphrey, lived in this house a few yards away from the Bell Inn.

A note of interest: The daughter of Thomas Pumphrey married Captain Philip Holtzerman of the 1st Light Battalion K.G.L., who was killed leading reinforcements into La Haye Sainte.

A *Barrack Hall*

B *Woodgate Farm*

C *Hanover House*

D *Goddard House*

E *The Bell Inn*

F *Thomas Pumphrey's House*

Records from St Peter's, Bexhill
by Janet Harris

BAPTISMS

Parents	Child's Name	Born	Baptised
1804			
ARGENTEN, Josef & Mary	Sarah	16th May	21st Oct
BOEG, Frederic & Christiana	Henrich Fdk. Gerlach		25th Nov
BRANDES, Frederich &	Albrecht Urbanus		
MYER, Louisa	Theodore	9th Sept	26th Sept
BRASSER, Toussaint & Marie	Frederic Joseph		5th Dec
GORLACH, Deidrich & Maria	Henrick Friedrich	25th Nov	16th Dec
HILBETCH, John & Doris	Doris Caroline		30th Sept
JHINES, Wm & Mary	Maria	2nd Dec	16th Dec
LINDHAUER, John & Phillis	Chas. Wm. Ferdinand		
SAACKE, Philip & Lucy	John George Henry		
	Christopher		2nd Dec
SCHIERTS, Pheleep & ??	Phoebe	18th Nov	18th Nov
SCHMIDT, Martin & Elizabeth	Luke	9th Oct	29th Oct★
SCHROEDER, Henry & Catherine	Francisca Mary Anne		
	Susannah		14th Oct
STAHL, Hans Christian & Hannah	Georg Christian	23rd Sept	25th Sept
STIEMETZ, Frederick & Justinia	Ernes		2nd Dec

★ Buried 31st October 1804

Parents	Child's Name	Born	Baptised
1805			
DENKENKAMP, Heinrich &	Ernest August		
Christina	Rudolf	12th Feb	
DUNKEL, Julius & Dorothea	Johanna Christina		
	Elizabeth	2nd June	20th June
FRANCK, Christian & Anna Louise	Charles Antoine		
	Ludwig		3rd Feb
HESSEN, David & Maria	Frederica Caroline		
	Marianne	4th June	16th June
HOLEBURG, John W & Johanna	Anna Margaretta	19th June	16th July
LUFFBORN/LUSSBORN, James	Anne	27th Oct	13th Jan
& Charlotte		1804	1805
MARKS, Joseph & Charlotte	Johanna Louisa		
	Charlotte	15th Aug	18th Aug

MECKER, Henry & Nancy	Johann Hendrich Friedrich		7th May
NAGEL, Adolphus & Eliza	Anna	23rd June	28th July
OELIZ, George A & Annie Sophia	Charles	24th March	7th April
PINKENBURGEN, John F & Sophia Dorothea	John Frederick Ernest		9th April
PODA, Christian & Doris	Fdch. Adam		12th May
SALTZ, Hendrich & Catherina	Hendrich Frederick Christian Ludwig	7th May	12th May
SOENTGEN, Sergeant & Caroline	Frederick Leopold Carl Sebastien		12th Mar
STEPHEN, Henry & Wilhelmina	Henry Wilhelm		24th Feb
TOURGON, Joseph & Agnes	Adam		7th May
UHLEEN, Johann & Maria	Johann Adolphus	13th June	20th Aug
WEGMEYER, Johann Adolph & ??	John Arthur	4th Jan	13th Jan
WEIBER, Wilhelm & Charlotte	Wilhelm	16th Dec 1804	20th Jan
WILBERG, Fdk. John & Anna Maria	Frederick	1st Oct	6th Oct

1806 – No baptisms recorded

1807

AUGOST, Uppa(?) & Elizabeth	Henrietta	15th Dec	20th Dec
DANKAERTS, John & Maria	John	9th June	20th July
SCHULTZ, Fdk. & Dorothea	Anna Elizabeth	18th Dec	25th Dec
WILHELM – No forenames	John Christian		13th Dec

1808

BECKER, Andreas & Catherine	Carolina		24th Jan
HILDERBRAND, Geo. & Dorothy	Johanna Frederika Wilhelmina	25th Dec 1807	10th Jan
KICHINEN, Christian & Maria	Caroline Dorothea	20th Mar	10th April
KOCH, Freidrich & Henrietta	Sarah Henrietta	5th Jan	17th Jan
LINDERMAN, Fdk. & Caroline	Caroline	20th Mar	10th Apr
MERTZ, Loncas & Maria M.	Maria Eliz. Anne	9th Jan	17th Jan
MULLER, Henry & Sophia	Frederich Henry	13th Feb	28th Feb

1809

EHEM, Christian & Anna	Geo. Charles	10th July	12th July
SCHARPER, Charles & Charlotte	William	11th Dec	30th Dec

1810

AMENDE, Fdk. & Carolina	Ernestine	20th Feb	11th Mar
DEMPEWELF, Henry & Isabella	Henry George	12th April	22nd April
DIEDERICH, Andrew & Bridget	Eliza	16th Nov	2nd Dec
DURING, Albrecht & Johanna	George Arp	17th Oct	1st Dec
GAPER, Jaques & Maria	John Antony	9th Aug	19th Aug
HESSE, Christopher & Ellinor	John George	21st Jan	28th Jan
KJRCHEN, Jacques & Maria	Caroline Albertine	28th Sept	7th Oct
RASEL, Wilhelm & Caroline	Wilhelmina Charlotte	31st Dec 1809	7th Jan
RONER, Charles & Katherine	Wilhelmina Amelia	25th July	9th Sept
SCHRODER, Henry & Grace	Henry	5th June	17th June
STOCKMAN, Frederick & Caroline	George Frederick Christian	26th Mar	1st April
THEILE, Frederich & Margaret	Anna Louise	12th May	3rd June
WARERS, Wilhelm & Johanna	Elizabeth	20th June	1st July

1811

BRANDES, Frederich & Louise	Johanna Frederika	21st Jan	3rd Feb
BRUNETTE, Conrad & Sophie	Christian Fdk. Hy.		17th Mar
DANNENBURG, Bernard & Harriet	Caroline	11th July	25th Aug
GASKA, Henry & Maria	George	18th Feb	4th Mar
HANEMANN, Henry & Lucy	Frederick Henry	27th Nov	8th Dec
HELSERRICH, Jno. & Anne	John	22nd Dec 1810	13th Jan
HERBST, Francis & Anne	Ernest Francis	28th Mar	28th April
JOHNGEN, Frederick & Caroline	Adam Adolphus	25th June	14th July
KEESE, Henry & Rosina Amelia	Louisa Dorothea Sophia	10th Jan	20th Jan
KENISSMAN, Louis & Juliana	Amelia	29th May	16th June
KESEMEYER, Fdk & Dorothea	Henrietta	30th Jan	10th Feb
LANGENHEINECKE, No forenames	Adelaide Eliza	/th Oct	10th Nov
PRESSNER, William & Elizabeth	William	6th Sept	22nd Sept
RUSSE, Jno & Eliza	Amelia Henrietta Elizabeth	17th May	2nd June
SCHALEBACH, Henry & Doris	George Louis	30th June	14th July
SENELMAYER, Fdk. & Anna	Anna Christiana	24th Feb	4th Mar
WILDBERG, Frederick & Hanna	Wilhelmina Sophia Louisa Maria	28th Sept	13th Oct

1812

EBERHART, Fdk. & Charlotte	Mary Dorothea	27th Feb	8th Mar
KEESE, William & Amelia	Gustavus	20th April	3rd May

KEITLE, Charles & Charlotte	Louisa	20th Jan	9th Feb
LENTH, Dirk & Biddy	Elizabeth	25th Dec	
		1811	5th Jan
MEYER, Henry & Elisabeth	Fdk. Thomas	21st Mar	12th April
MEYER, Peter & Elisabeth	Maria Louisa		
There appears to be a missing page			
SCHRADER, Henry & Grace	John James	25th June	19th July
SCHUTZ, Christopher & Mary	Christopher	26th July	2nd Aug
SONDER, Christian & Leonora	Adolphus	5th Jan	19th Jan
SYMPHER, Jacob Augustus & Caroline Fredericka	Caroline Eliza		20th Sept
TATJE, Christopher & Elizabeth	William	15th Feb	15th Mar
von WINDHEIM, Anton Charles	Ernest Charles		
& Susannah	George	22nd Mar	19th April
WARTZ, Henry & Louisa	Henry	25th May	7th June
WELTEN, Frederick & Margaret	Juliana Maria	6th Oct	1st Nov
WENNERHOLM, Benjamin & Rachel	George William	26th Aug	20th Sept

Baptisms for 1813 & 1814 – no birth dates – just baptismal dates.

1813

BEHR, Christian & Catherine	Henry A.	14th Nov
BELL, Laurence & Elizabeth	Laurence	20th April
BITTER, Francis & Magdalen	Charles Francis	31st Oct
BRANDES, Frederick & Louisa	Jeanette Wilhelmina	13th June
BRAZIER, Sophia	Victor★	16th May
DELAFARQUE, William & Louise Maria	William James	7th Mar
DELTENHOEFER, Anton & Martha	Frederick Edward	19th April
DIEDRICH, Andrew & Bridget	Mary Anne	20th June
DUTISCHE, Pierre & Frances	Caroline	1st April
ENGENHAUSEN, George & Hannah	John Henry	12th Sept
FERMESTER, John D & Frederica	John Christian	25th July
GERKE, William & Dora	Francis	20th June
GERKE, Mary	John★	4th July
HEIMBRUCH, Ann Mary	Anne★	13th June
HEINRICHES, Frederick & Sophia	Sophia Louise	31st Oct
HINE, Henry G and Mary A	Henry George	1st Aug

IBELING, Henry & Sophia	Augustus Louis	
KERSCHE, John & Mary	John Henry Frederick	20th April
LANGENBERG, William & Maria	John Peter	2nd May
LUTTER, George & Mary	Henry George	10th Oct
MEYER, Henry & Hannah	Henrietta Marianna	28th Mar
MULLEN, William & Ann	Frederick	6th June
MULLER, Gabriel & Louise	George Frederick	4th July
REGEN, Louis & Sophia	Frederick Ernest Conrad	6th June
SARVAEN, Michael & Hannah	Hannah D F	28th Nov
SATLER, James & Catherine	John Frederick	17th Oct
SCHNEDER, John & Doris	Charles Henry	31st Oct
SCHULENBORG, Louis & Margaret	Mary	27th June
SENDER, Henry & Esther	Henry Louis	23rd May
STANLEY, Francis & Sophia	Dorothea Leonore	23rd May
VONDERBURG, Henry & Sophia	Wilhelmia Sophia	26th Dec
WARNECKE, Frederick & Martha	Mary Louisa	5th Sept

★ Illegitimate

1814

BESSELMAN, Frederick & Mary	Sophia Louisa	13th Feb
BOMKAPEL, Christian & Doris	John	9th Jan
CRIPMAN, William & Louisa	Sophia Louise	17th July
FISCHER, Frederick & Sophia	Sophia Henrietta	1st May
HARTZE, Frederick & Annie Louise	Charles Frederick Henry	15th May
LUTTERMAN, Frederick & Catherine	Ludwig	26th June
	Sophia Doris	26th June
MEYER, Henry & Hannah	Sophia Louisa	1st May
MEYER, Henry & Sophia	Henry Gottleib	10th July
RUNDE, Frederick & Leonora	John Henry	17th April
SCHAEFER, Frederick & Anna	Frederick	20th Feb
STEINCKE, William & Priscilla	Priscilla Selina	30th Jan
WIEGREBE, Frederick & Maria	Frederick Leopold	3rd July

MARRIAGES

1804

BULTITUDE, William	Margaret Bigsby	10th December
BUSCHE, August	Ann Steel	21st December
HENNES, John	Sarah Jones	27th August
HERLE, Adolphus	Sophia Marlene Mecker	31st December
HUTTERSEN, Christian	Mary Ann Wolfen	11th September
SUIR, Frederick	Anna Catherine Jales	31st December
WEIL, John	Catherine Beesen	1st October
WITZ, William	Sarah Daniels	3rd September

1805

ALLTMAN (?), John	Marianne Bessin	29th April
AUSTIN, Samuel	Elisabet Erans (?)	4th December
FISCHER, Charles Frederick	Joan Bradley	19th September
HEISEL, Freidrich	Caroline Dearsen	7th October
LORG, John Frederick	Justine Appelin	29th April
MONTAG, George	Dorothea Ohlemann	1st October
SCHNEIDER, Josef	Martha Geitz	13th August
SCHRADER, Louis	Wilhelmina Kessler	20th August

1806

DANKAERT, John	Maria Thomas	26th June

1807

ALRUTZ, Frederick	Frederica Mons	21st December
FUCHS, Charles	Anna Knudsen	21st December
GUNTER, William	Ann Hall	7th October
HEINZIG, Fdk. Leopold	Johanna Sophia Louise Werther	1st December

1808 – No marriages recorded

1809

DERDERICH, Andreas	Biddy Canagan	25th June
LANGE, Henry	Maria Carlsson	13th May
STOCKMEYER, Frederick	Caroline Bachhaus	9th July

1810

BUSCH, Henry	Harriet Haselden	24th September
BUSSKE (?), John	Ilse Bewing	29th September
EBELING, Henry	Sophia Niewisch	7th May

GRAEBE, Louis	Maria Mange	4th March
NORDMAN, Frederic	Frederica Maeys	18th February
RAUCH, Henry	Hannah Wild	9th October
SCHACKENBACH, Henry	Dorothy Behrens	11th June
SCHAEFFER, Adam	Mary Harmer	24th December
SLAPER, Jacques	Nina Vanessa	29th January
SUPEKE, Henry Joachim	Frances Vourlon	4th February

1811

BERGMAN, Frederick	Sarah Evans	14th October
HUNDERMARK, Frederick	Amelia Erchnieyer	6th June
SCHAFER, Adam	Mary Fitzpatrick	24th December
TUMMSEL (?), William	Philadelphia Dann	11th February
WERNERHOLME, Benjamin	Rachel Cramp	3rd June

1812

BABOTZ (?), Francis	Sarah Tutton	1st June
DALINGBURG, Frederick	Sarah Witz	13th November
DUTISCHE, Pierre	Frances Ford	17th August
HAIMBS, Frederick	Catherine Gatehoff	9th November
HEUTGEN, Ludwig	Doris Moabrauern (?)	15th June
HOLTZERMAN, Philip	Mary Ann Pumphrey	6th January
KLEINENZ, Louis	Harriet Deeprose	28th August
LOSCHING, Francis	Hannah Ochling	20th July
PINNSK, Josef	Hannah Rollason	5th February
SCHIEURBRANDT, Thomas	Sarah Perkins	9th November
STANCKE, Francis	Sophia Schluter	21st May
WETZIG, Gottleib	Sarah Hayes	9th June

1813

ACHERMANN, Godfrey	Catherine Sylvan	24th May
CONRAD, Ignatz	Louise Maynard	29th June
CONRADI, Henry	Hannah Baker	2nd April
FRANZ, Martin	Lucy Timson	20th June
HEII'JE, George	Mary Ann Burt	4th January
HENNE, John	Rose Dogherty	16th August
MARTHIES, Henry	Hannah Haselden	3rd May
RICH, William	Mary Maplesden	17th August
ROMANOWSKI, Valentin	Marianna Deschiska	11th July
RUBEIN, Lorenz	Mary Ann Groombridge	1st June
SATLER, Jacob	Catherine Weishoff	6th June
SCHIMPF, Zacharia	Ann Smith	26th December
SUTTER, Charles Joseph	Frances Rich	18th January

SUTTER, Corporal George	Maddalen Mertz	17th May
TERRUP, Henry	Catherine Heintrenter	19th December

1814

ANDREAS, David	Rebecca Eden	18th July
ASCHENBACH, John	Jemima Davis	1st August
DEGEN, Frederick	Maria de Lonsch	30th January
DOLGER, Frederick	Mary Ann Trueman	11th February
FISCHER, William	Anne Tibbett	10th January
HETTENHIAUSER, Henry	Alice Senden	6th June
HOLTZHAUSER, Henry	Sophia Beckett	18th July
KEHRES, Henry	Dorothea Martzen	16th May
LINGE, Charles	Eleanor Heine	13th February
LORISCHE, Charles	Joanna Schilling	7th August
LUDEWIGE, Charles	Emma Cook	25th July
MARTENS, Antony	Dorothea Olderfeldt	16th May
MEYER, Ulric	Catherine Tappe	27th May
MULLER, George	Elizabeth Timms	25th January
SCHIELS, Henry	Dorothea Neimeyer	11th July
SMITH, Frederick William	Sophia Wiswe	17th May
WIEGREBE, Frederick	Maria Heise	14th August

BURIALS

	Buried	Age
1804		
AN HANOVERIAN SOLDIER		
IMMANHAUSER, William	3rd September	24
SCHIMIIDT, Luke	31st October	Infant
SIEURSER, Uhle	19th December	26
SIEURSER, Mrs Shadwell	19th December	26
THOTZENIIAUSEN, ??	7th August	23
1805		
A GERMAN	18th July	–
A GERMAN	7th September	–
EZLMES, "Soldier"	4th July	21
HIELMZTS, Carolina	6th July	5 months
JAGOR, August	7th March	28
MELDAU, Henry	7th January	24
MIAS, William	12th March	28
OBRUGGE, Christopher	7th May	28

| SCHERANDES, "Drummer" | 8th May | 23 |

None recorded for 1806

1807
| AUGUSTIN, Frederick | 20th December | 11 months |

1808
A GERMAN INFANT	24th April	
CHRISTIAN, Peter	10th January	10 months
HORSGEST, Henry	21st January	Infant

1809
APFELSTED, Anne	29th May	34
CHRISTINA, Johanna	24th April	1
HESSE, Henry	13th May	28
MEARING, Conrad	24th March	23
PROSTE, Frederick	28th April	25
SCHLETZE, Frederick	20th May	23
SCHLICHTING, Christopher	9th May	25
VILLIAMAGE, Martha	22nd March	–
VOLHOM, John	11th April	1

1810
BRODMAN, Frederick	14th June	30
DIEFENBERG, Godfrey	12th April	25
CRUGER (or KRUGER?)	1st September	22
FERGER, George	29th January	25
GRASSE, Frederick	20th January	26
GRAUMANN, Henry	2nd March	26
GOOTFORD (?), Girboth	24th March	21
GROSSCOTT, Christian	22nd June	37
HEGERMAN, Amstci	22nd February	30
HUGELBERG, Peter	10th March	32
KLAMIIVIAN, George	31st January	22
LUBITSKY, John	30th September	27
MULLER, William	26th March	Infant
OTMAN, Frederick	6th May	28
OTTER, George	4th April	26
RIEG, Cornelius	3rd June	22
SCHONENHEDEN, John	10th January	25
SHOULDSTER, Peter	18th March	26
VOSSE, Jonathan	7th April	21

1811

HUNDERMARK, ??	12th November	Infant
WATISNOFF, Francis	22nd November	26

1812

BUSCHMAN, Frederick	27th November	30
KRUGER, Henry	5th June	26
LEPP, John Frederick	24th December	Infant
MESSE, Conrad	3rd August	25
SCHUTZ, Christopher	8th August	Infant
TATJE, Elizabeth	27th May	23
VANDAMMIE, Herman	29th November	30

1813

ALTENHAFER, Franco	25th July	34
BAUMGARTNER, Francis	3rd February	30
BECKER, Andrew	18th December	46
BECKER, Augustus	17th March	72
BOCKELMAN, Frederick	24th March	34
DEPO, Francis	2nd September	23
DRIER, Mary	21st March	Infant
FERNER, Christian	12th April	23
KLUSSMEYER, Godfrey	17th January	27
MEYER, Henry Manana	13th April	Infant
MIRZ, Elizabeth Maria	8th April	3
MULLER, John	28th December	Infant
REBENSHAUR, Frederick	14th October	28
REGER, Henry	21st June	Infant
ROCKER, Frederick	26th April	28
SCHUCHAID, Godfrey	16th November	43
WALRUP, Balthasar	26th April	39
TERRUP, Henry	11th April	1

1814

BERCHERDING, Frederick	3rd February	29
DEMITZ, Charles	7th January	44
FISCHER, Frederick	11th February	45
FLORNING, Valentine	14th August	60
FRESE, John	10th January	45
GEORGESED, John Xtian	4th August	Infant
GERHE, Frederick	14th January	34
JANECHE, Philip	20th January	42
KELLNER, Henry	14th May	32

KELLNER, John	13th January	57
KLEINE, William	12th April	33
KUHLMAN, George	10th February	31
KUHINE, Peter	18th May	30
MILCHAL, Mary	31st August	28
SANDER, Charles	31st July	30
VOLGRAF, Conrad	1st February	41
WELLINGS, Clemens	12th April	40

1815
SCHIES, Hans	16th May	40

1820
SCHANMANN, Jeanette	7th September	33

1835
OLDERHAUSEN, Mercy	14th April	51

A Guided Walk Around Bexhill Old Town

For the visitor, a stroll through Bexhill Old Town can be a very pleasant experience, recalling life in a more leisurely age. The places of interest relating to the King's German Legion are, in the main, freely accessible; people of more advanced years might like to know that there are a couple of short but fairly steep inclines to negotiate.

By the Manor Gardens off De La Warr Road there is an adequate free car park with public conveniences. Walk up the ramp out of the car park and turn left and almost opposite, on the other side of the road, you will see numbers 5 and 7, the one-time home of the Customs Officer, Thomas Pumphrey, whose daughter, as already mentioned elsewhere in this book, married Captain Philip Holtzerman of the 1st Light Battalion K.G.L.

Further left, you will see the Bell Inn which stands at the bottom of Church Street. Cross over and go up Church Street, noting on the left the period houses which adjoin the Inn, built by a previous owner to accommodate some of the influx of soldiers. On the right is the lych gate which leads into the churchyard and a few yards in, to the left of the path, is a stone to the memory of Ann, the wife of Captain Turner of the Royal Wagon Train. Further in, on the right, are three stones together, that on the left being to Robert White of the 11th Light Dragoons, drowned in 1804 whilst exercising his horse on the beach; "On duty Cheerful and in Battle Brave, Yet fell a Victim to the foaming Wave".

The stone next to his is now virtually unreadable but close inspection will still reveal the Masonic Insignia at the top. It is believed to be the grave of Drill Sergeant William Morrison who died in 1806. Behind the church a further stone commemorating another death in 1806, serves to remind us that life was perhaps harder and unhappier in those days, "Sacred to the memory of Mary Jennings the Infant daughter of Captain Jennings 40th Regiment who departed this life on the 26th day of January 1806. Aged 16 weeks."

From the Church, continue along Church Street, around the left hand bend into Short Lane and go down the hill★ to the T-junction (Chantry Lane). Turn right, walk under the by-pass and the first turning on the left is Barrack Road.

---

* Almost at the bottom of the hill, on the left, is a stone wall with protuberances (mounting blocks). These would have been used by the K.G.L. and others for mounting their horses. Former stables, 19th/20th century, were situated opposite the west door of the Church.

On the right hand side of Barrack Road is the site of the old cemetery, commemorated by the signboard placed there by the Hanoverian Study Group (together with the Old Town Preservation Society) of Bexhill-on-Sea. The earliest Barracks were along the right side of Barrack Road and extended down to what is now London Road.

Retrace your steps to the church. On the way you will meet two of the short inclines mentioned earlier. The return route under the by-pass is quite steep and the left turn up into Church Street presents an even steeper aspect but, fortunately, on the corner is a bench seat providing a welcome rest between the two. Resist the temptation to avoid Church Street by going straight on to the village because the road further on becomes very narrow and is without pavements.

Return to the Bell Inn and from there proceed beneath the clock before turning right into High Street. On the opposite side of the road is Hanover House, which is believed to have been owned initially by a German officer. At the far end of High Street was, until recently, the premises of Pocock's, which used to supply meat to the King's German Legion. To reach Barrack Hall, cross with care Chantry Lane. Alternatively, retrace your steps and cross by the pillar box, walking on the yellow lines to the bollarded junction.

By taking the public footpath to the left of the Hall, the lane can be seen and entered leading to the old parade ground*, now allotments. Note the beech tree in the grounds of Barrack Hall; its estimated age at the time of the Barracks being 100 years. Return to the road and turn right along Belle Hill. On the left you will find Goddard House, where it is believed the commanding officer of the King's German Legion, Major General Sir Charles Alten, lived.

This ends the short tour of the village and it only remains for the visitor to return via the High Street to the car park.

For visitors' information, there is a pleasant cafe/restaurant "The Walnut Tree", in the High Street. There one can relax in pleasant surroundings with morning coffee/tea and home-made cakes, or indeed enjoy a lunch. Of course, there is The Bell Inn. The Manor Gardens are worth a visit and are very attractive, with plenty of seats. The remains of the Manor House itself still exist, adding to the evocative and tranquil atmosphere.

---

* To make a good firm marching surface, the K.G.L. brought up shingles and flints from the beaches.

A Map of Bexhill Today

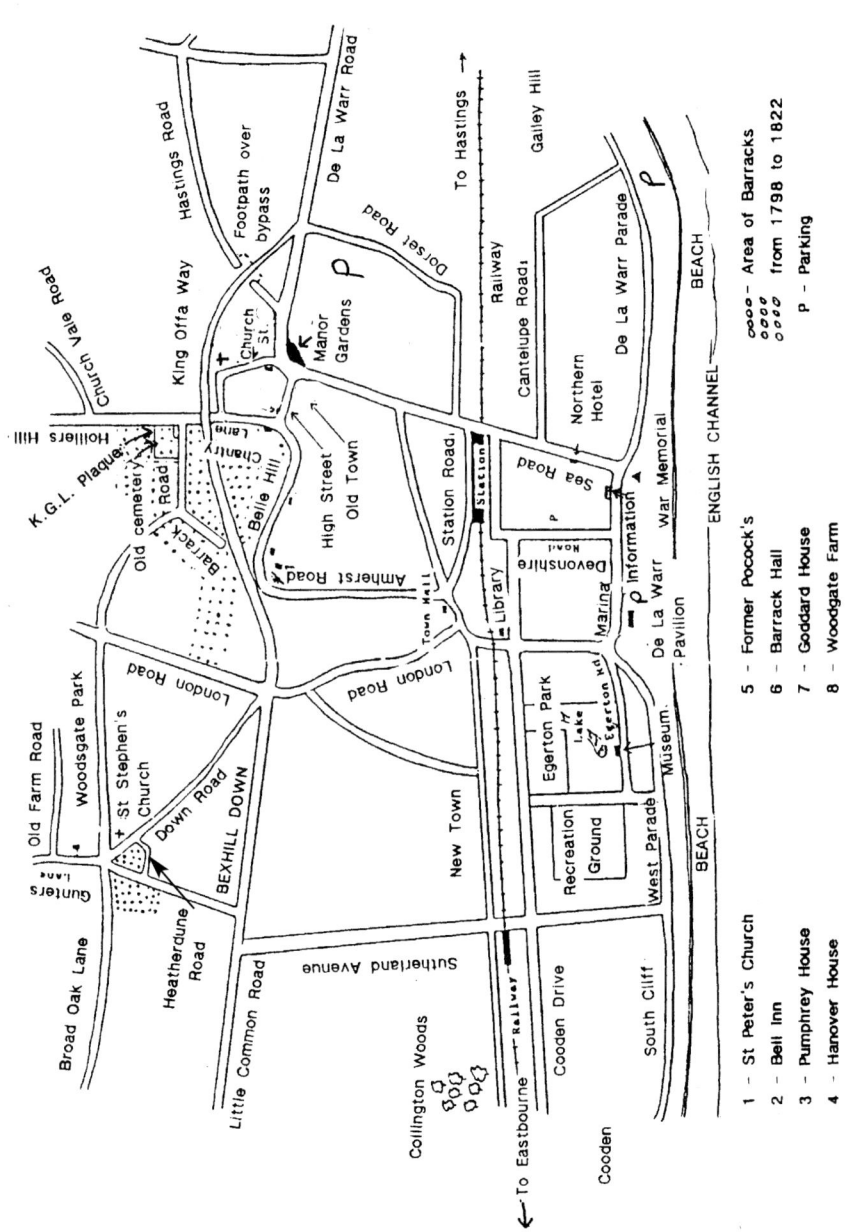

Legend:

oooo - Area of Barracks
oooo   from 1798 to 1822
oooo

P - Parking

1 - St Peter's Church
2 - Bell Inn
3 - Pumphrey House
4 - Hanover House
5 - Former Pocock's
6 - Barrack Hall
7 - Goddard House
8 - Woodgate Farm

IN-DEPTH READING REGARDING
THE KING'S GERMAN LEGION

1. At Waterloo
2. Walcheren
3. Command and Staff
4. Usual Rank of Commanders
5. Order of Battle – (ORBAT) – Waterloo

Waterloo

The defence of the farmhouse of La Haye Sainte during the Battle of Waterloo was a decisive factor in the success of Wellington's victory on 18th June 1815 as follows:-

"Wellington posted a detachment of the King's German Legion, who were well known for their reliability, at La Haye Sainte where they spent an uncomfortable night in wet conditions. At 3pm the next day, the French attacked, but this was repulsed. The K.G.L., who were by then very short of ammunition, made repeated requests for more supplies, but to no avail. The dead and wounded were searched for ammunition but the result was only 4–5 rounds per man. The French made another attack. After a valiant attempt to fight off the invading French, the K.G.L.'s ammunition was exhausted and the farm had to be abandoned. The French broke in and a fierce fight took place with bayonets and rifle butts. Only 41 of the 350 Hanoverians reached the crossroads."

On 18th June 1998, a group of the Bexhill Hanoverian Study Group visited Waterloo to attend the official ceremony of the dedication of a commemorative plaque, placed on the wall of La Haye Sainte to the 2nd Light Battalion of the King's German Legion, who defended the farm at the Battle of Waterloo on 18th June 1815.

The words on the plaque (in English) are as follows:-

> TO MAJ. BARING AND THE 2ND LIGHT
> Btn. KGL's HEROIC DEFENCE OF
> LA HAIE SAINTE 18 JUNE 1815
> ALSO TO COL. von OMPTEDA WHO FELL
> LEADING A BRAVE COUNTER-ATTACK
> AFTER THE FALL OF THE FARM
>
> DEDICATED BY
> BEXHILL-ON-SEA ENGLAND
> A KING'S GERMAN LEGION
> GARRISON 1804–14

This was a great achievement for the Bexhill Hanoverian Study Group. However, they were very grateful to various people and organisations who gave donations towards the project.

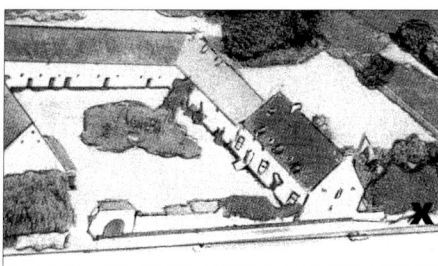

Aerial view of La Haye Sainte. The cross denotes the position of the commemorative plaque. At this spot, behind the wall, is where Colonel von Ompteda fell when leading a counter-attack after the fall of the farm.

The Commemorative Plaque, complete with coloured logos, both of the Bexhill Coat of Arms and the BHSG's own emblem.

N.B. La Haye Sainte, which was repaired soon after the Battle of Waterloo, has not changed since , except for the heavy traffic. It is still a working farm.

Some names on the Hanoverian Monument at La Haye Sainte

The Hanoverian Monument was erected in 1818 to commemorate the defenders of La Haye Sainte. It also marks the site of one of the graves on the battlefield, a huge pit where 4,000 were buried.

Lieutenant Anton Albert – 1st Battalion, K.G.L. – killed

Captain Adol. Bosewiel (Major) – 2nd Light Battalion, K.G.L. killed

Major G. Chuden – 4th Line Battalion, K.G.L. – died of wounds

Ensign Edward T. Cronhelm – 4th Line Battalion, K.G.L. – killed

Captain Frederick Didel – 3rd Line Battalion, K.G.L. – killed

Captain Alexander Goeben – 1st Light Battalion, K.G.L. – killed

Captain Charles von Holle – 2nd Light Battalion, K.G.L. – killed

Captain Philip Holtzermann – 1st Light Battalion, K.G.L. – killed

Lieutenant William Marenholtz – 8th Line Battalion, K.G.L. – killed

Captain Henry Marschalck 1st Light Battalion, K.G.L. – killed

Colonel Baron Christian von Ompteda – Commanded the 2nd K.G.L. Infantry Brigade – killed – *see memorial (plaque) to Baring on previous page.*

Ensign Frederick Robertson – 2nd Light Battalion, K.G.L. – killed

Captain William Schaumann – 2nd Light Battalion, K.G.L. – killed

Adjutant John Lewis Schuck – 5th Line Battalion, K.G.L. – killed

Captain George Tilee – 2nd Line Battalion, K.G.L. killed

Captain Augustus William von Voigt – 8th Line Battalion – killed

Captain Thilo von Westernhagen – 8th Line Battalion – killed

Captain Christian von Wurmb – 5th Line Battalion, K.G.L. – killed

Hanoverian Monument

La Haye Sainte

Major George Baring (and Colonel Ompteda) in the defence of La Haye Sainte: 18th June 1815:- Extracts taken from "The History of the King's German Legion" by N. Ludlow Beamish.

Re-enactment of the Battle of La Haye Sainte

"... In the early afternoon, during the conflict of Waterloo, a division of the French army attacked the farm of La Haye Sainte. This important post, situated about mid-way between the contending armies ... was entrusted to the second light battalion of the King's German Legion, under the command of Major Baring ... this consisted of six companies amounting, inclusive of sergeants, to three hundred and seventy-six men. Of these, Major Baring posted three companies in the orchard, two in the buildings and one in the rear garden ... the small detachment in the orchard fell back into the barn when attacked by overpowering numbers of French troops ... later the French took possession of the garden driving the legion company (including reinforcements of the light battalion Luneburg under Colonel von Klencke) into the buildings and the Germans suffered a severe loss in officers and men. ... Of Baring's battalion the greater part reached the main position; the rest secured themselves in the farmyard and buildings. ...

"The combat continued at La Haye Sainte. ... At about five o'clock, an attack was made by a preponderating force of not less than three divisions of the French army. ... Baring's soldiers met the onset with firmness, levelling their trusty rifles with certain aim against the enemy, every bullet took effect. ... The open gateway being a weak point, the assailants seemed confident of being able to force in, but the little garrison knew its value and not an opening was given. Man after man was bayoneted by Baring's unyielding soldiers at this gateway, until the slain actually formed a rampart for the assailants, but no entrance was given and the furious contest continued to rage.

Major Baring, having examined the state of ammunition found it low and immediately sent an officer with a request for a fresh supply. But no rifle ammunition was to be had; the cart which should have brought it was upset in the general confusion and no other means of supply was at hand. This calamity was unknown to Major Baring and, some time having elapsed without the expected arrival, he despatched another officer to the rear with the same request, and a third was sent.

However two hundred Nassau troops were added to the numbers of the little garrison and the struggle raged on. ... The assailants gave up hope of being able to effect an entrance into the buildings by direct assault and set the barn on fire ... although water was available, all means of conveying it had been broken up. Baring, observing the large cooking kettles carried by the Nassau troops, filled one with water; officers and men followed this example and, facing almost certain destruction, carried the water to the flaming barn and the fire was eventually extinguished, but many a brave man had fallen and many more, covered with wounds, continued to expose themselves with a degree of devotion beyond all praise. ...

More than an hour passed and the French, tired from fruitless attack, fell back. The relief given to the Germans may well be imagined but on counting the remaining cartridges Baring found that the men had not, on an average, more than from three to four each! ... The French columns again closed upon the farm ... however every shot fired by the defenders rendered their situation more critical ... the fire of the defenders gradually diminished ... and the French mounted the roof and walls and Baring reluctantly gave the order to retire from the yard into the rear garden. The house now being in the hands of the enemy, Baring therefore directed the men to retire to the main position; with the remnant of his brave followers, he joined the first light battalion in the hollow road behind the farm. ...

Here combat again raged; many officers and men struck down ... a column of French cavalry having debouched from La Haye Sainte, Sir Charles Alten sent Colonel Ompteda directions to deploy, if possible, the fifth battalion and attack the column. Ompteda represented that such a movement could not be made without a useless sacrifice of men. ... At this moment the Prince of Orange rode up and ordered Colonel Ompteda to deploy; on the same representations being made to his royal highness, he impatiently repeated the order upon which Ompteda instantly mounted his horse, gave the fatal word of command and led forward the battalion. His gallant men jumped cheerfully over the ravine and fell upon the French column with a loud hurrah! the column gave way and fled but enemy horsemen rushed from the ambuscade, thundered down upon the flank; Ompteda was killed and about one hundred and thirty sergeants and soldiers were struck down. ...

The light battalions of the legion had also been forced back; a third horse had been killed under Major Baring and falling upon him, nearly deprived him of the use of his leg; he managed however to creep to a farmhouse, where he was assisted onto another horse and sought the remains of his brave battalion."

A British 9-pounder gun and limber first introduced during the Peninsula Campaign.

N.B. (The day closed with the gallant Major Baring – whom we left in search of the remnant of his brave battalion, "and after riding sometime in an almost distracted state of mind, smarting from the pain of his wound – was informed they had been obliged to leave the field from the want of ammunition and soon afterwards the cry of 'Victory' met his ear; the allied line advanced. Baring, now having no men to command, joined the first hussars of the legion and with them, followed the enemy in the final pursuit).

The 3rd Hussars of The King's German Legion is depicted in the above illustration, with the line and light infantry of the Legion.
Aquatint by I.C Stadler after Charles Hamilton Smith, published April 1815

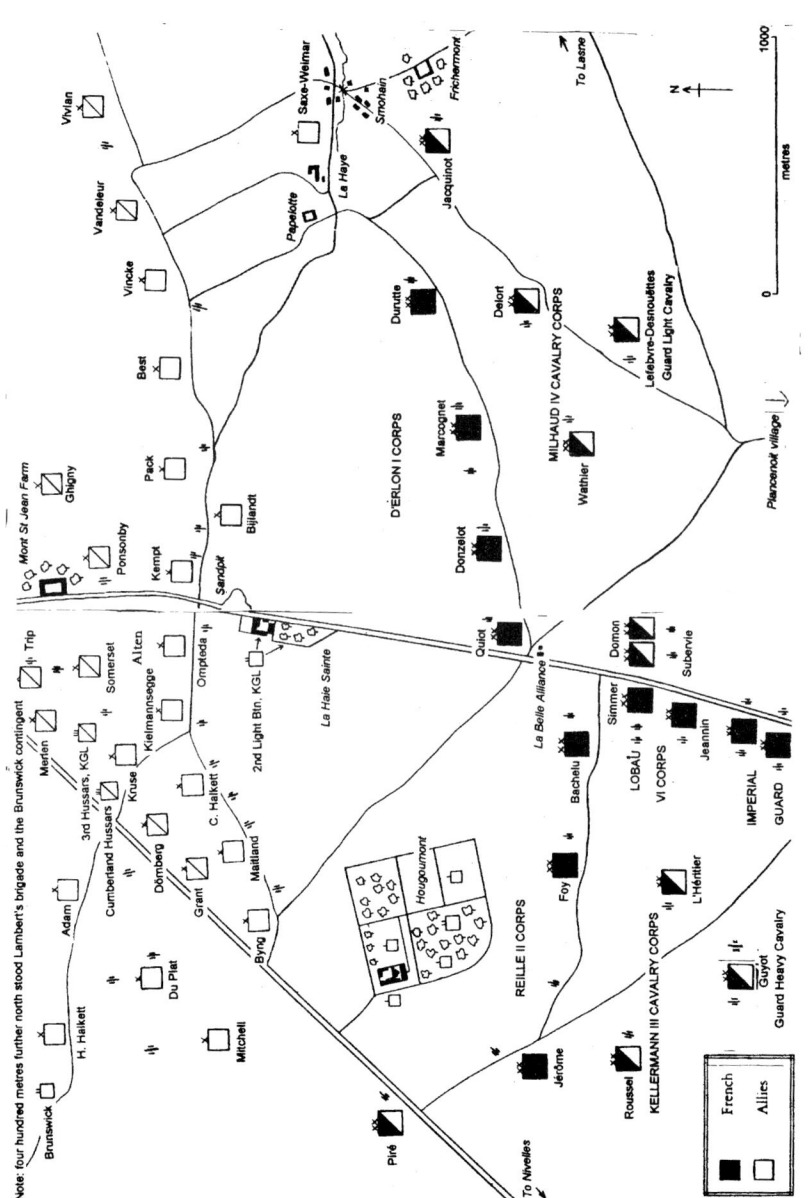

The Battlefield of Waterloo: 11.30am, 18th June (about the time of the first shot by Napoleon)

Hougoumont

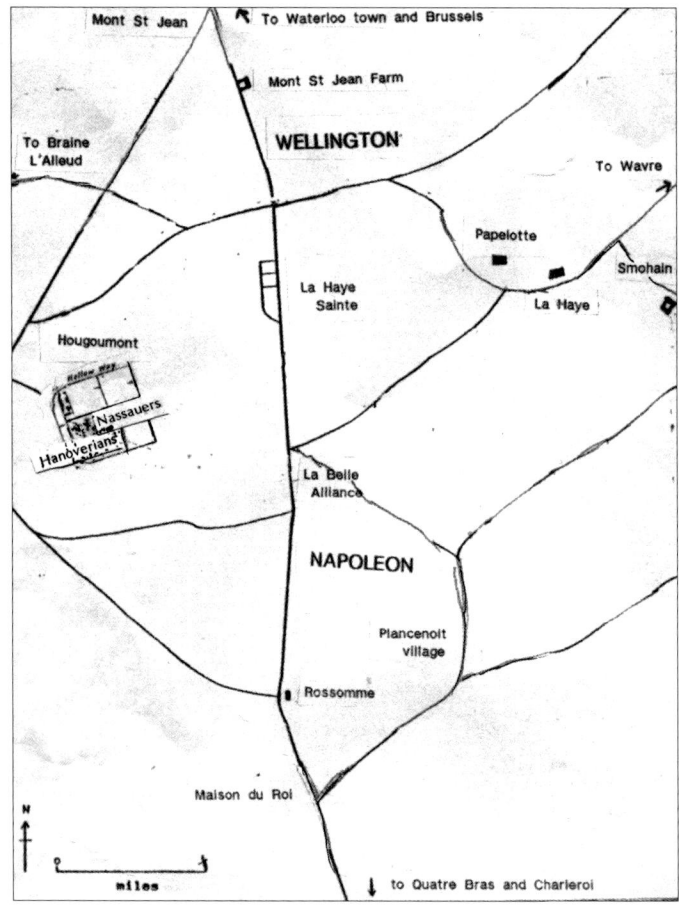

Map showing position of La Haye Sainte on the battlefield.

At the opening of the conflict (around 11.30am) Hougoumont was attacked. At this time, the orchard to the south of the farm was defended by Nassauers (Belgian/Dutch troops) and Hanoverian★ sharpshooters (Jägers).

Other detachments★★ of the K.G.L, including cavalry, fought along Wellington's line of defence during the Battle.

★ Not necessarily K.G.L. More likely that they were newly formed units of the Electorate of Hanover.
★★See 'Order of Battle – (ORBAT) Waterloo' (pages 67-75).

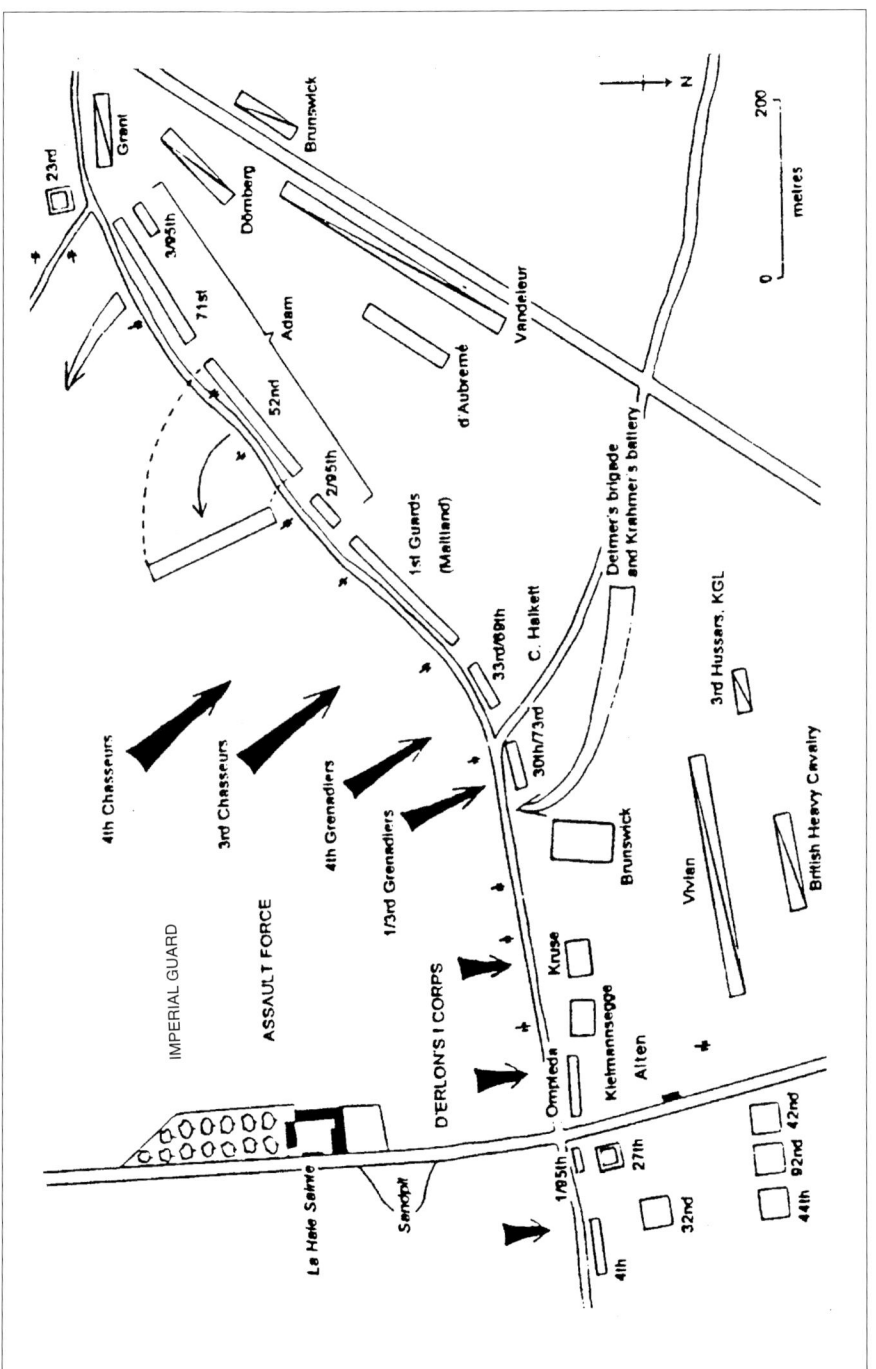

Repulse of Imperial Guard (Approx. 7.30–8.00pm)

Walcheren

The worst expedition of the Napoleonic wars was the British landing in the Low Countries in 1809; the British hoped to assist the Austrians, who had gone to war against the French, and to destroy the French fleet, thought to be in Flushing.

The British force of over 39,000 men – including units of the King's German Legion – began to land in Walcheren on 30th July. This force was larger than the British force in Portugal under Wellington. By the time the troops had landed, the Austrians had been defeated and were negotiating a peace treaty with Napoleon. Although the British had captured Flushing the French had moved their fleet to Antwerp, thus denying the British any chance of destroying it.

By December 1809, the last British troops had been withdrawn from Walcheren. The British force suffered 4,066 deaths during the expedition, yet only 106 officers and men were killed in combat. The rest died from Walcheren Fever. On 1st February 1810, a staggering 11,513 officers and men were still carried on the rolls as sick. Less than two years later, many of these troops were still so weakened by the disease that Wellington requested that no unit that had served in the Walcheren Campaign be sent to him.

Additional information: From Walcheren, many units of soldiers, including those of the King's German Legion, were brought back to England where large numbers died of the fever.

Some of the King's German Legion soldiers who died of the Walcheren fever are buried in Barrack Road Cemetery, Bexhill.

Command and Staff

Edited and translated by Michael A. Taenzer
(by kind permission of Mr. Taenzer)

Structure of Command

The meaning of the English designation "King's German Legion", shortened to K.G.L. is best reflected in the German "Königlich Deutsche Legion". ... The officers of the Legion themselves used the designation "Königlich Grosbrittanisch-Deutsche Legion" which can be found on the monument for their comrades, who were killed on the battlefield of Waterloo. Later "Königlich Deutsche Legion" became the official designation in the Hannoverian army, which is proved by the inscriptions on the Waterloo Column in Hannover. ...

The Legion never served as a tactically independent body under its own commander; they were merged with English units to form larger formations.

With the English units, the Legion was also part of the army under the British Commander-in-Chief. In England where, by law, the sovereign was above every institution of the country, he was not allowed to serve at the head of any of them. Hence, the king could not be Commander-in-Chief of the army himself. Therefore, from 1798 this post was filled by the Duke of York, one of the king's sons. His right hand was the Secretary AT War, who represented the Commander-in-Chief in Parliament and obtained the necessary funds from the latter. So both of them were not completely free in their actions. Additionally, the Secretary of the Navy and the Admiralty were responsible for naval transports. Another institution of a more technical nature was the Board of Ordnance, with its Master General of Ordnance (formed in 1806), who was responsible for Artillery, Engineers, Materiel of War, Barracks, etc. This department also depended upon the funds of the Secretary OF War. Orders came from army headquarters at Horse Guards in Whitehall, London.*

---

* Note of interest: (Circa 1740) Barracks for Horse Guards were built on King Henry VIII's Jousting Ground.

Horse Guards today

The Legion itself as an organisational unit was led unified by its chief, Adolphus, Duke of Cambridge (seventh son of King George III) in everything relating to recruiting, subsistence and advancement, but in every other respect used in separate parts as necessary. The chief's right hand was a Chief Adjutant (Friedrich Count von der Decken). The adjutants of higher commands (divisions, brigades) were called brigade majors. They were selected by the commanders of those commands mostly because of personal trust. The number of brigade majors within the Legion alternated between 6 and 9. The English commander had an aide-de-camp from the Legion with him, if elements of the K.G.L. were among his troops. Officers of the general staff in the modern sense did not exist in the Legion. These duties were discharged by the Quartermaster General, the Assistant Quartermaster General and several Deputy Assistant Quartermaster Generals in the English army.

The Officers. Mostly the officers of the King's German Legion came from the disbanded army of the Electorate of Hannover. At the beginning, there were such large numbers that many officers could not be appointed, as corresponding units did not exist at the time. Before the end of 1803, 135 officers arrived in England and the British government granted them two-thirds of their pay until their final appointments. The substitution of officers during the existence of the Legion was always more than needed. ...

There were no generals in the modern sense. The highest officers of the Legion, regardless of their rank as general, were appointed as the colonel commandant of some regiment or battalion and ordered to command a division or brigade from time to time. ...

The uniforms of generals and staff consisted of scarlet coats with dark blue and gold embroidered collars and facings, long tails to coats with white facings, two rows of gold buttons with the royal cypher and crown. For dress occasions generals wore embroidered aiguillettes; the different ranks were only distinguished by different embroidery on the collar, or on the body of coats. Off-duty generals and staff wore simple blue coats with gold buttons. The trousers were white leather or linen. Half height Hessian boots with screw-on spurs were worn. The dress sash was gold-red, for service the same red silk as for all the army, sword knots of the same colour. A cocked hat with black cockade, gold-red and hanging white feathers completed the dress; caps did not exist. The sabre in steel scabbard was worn on a golden or dark red belt. Overcoats were blue, shabraques red with gold borders. (Shabraques were a type of ornamental rug worn over the saddle of the horse.)

The insignia of generals were aiguillettes and chevrons. The field officers wore epaulettes with fringes on both shoulders, the captains wore one only on the right shoulder. The hussars and the light battalions did not have these distinctions. The subalterns wore yellow and white metal wings, the men of the heavy dragoons and all the infantry had woollen wings. The rank of non-commissioned officers was distinguished by gold or silver chevrons on the right upper sleeve. The sergeant major had four with a crown above, the sergeant three, the quartermaster sergeant and the cadet two, the corporal one. Non-commissioned officers were not saluted by the men when off duty.

Every regiment or battalion of the Legion had an adjutant, an officer as quartermaster and a paymaster. Besides the paperwork, unless this was the responsibility of the paymaster or the quartermaster, the adjutants were responsible for the drill exercises, assisted by the sergeant majors. On several occasions non-commissioned officers with a good knowledge of the duties, were appointed adjutants if they could understand English. The paymasters were generally native Englishmen. Like the quartermasters, they had the rank of officers and belonged in the mess.

The medical officers were nearly all from Hannover, forming a body of special ability. Bandsmen assisted them in their work by transporting the medical supplies. The regimental veterinary surgeons came mostly from the army of the Electorate of Hannover, returning in 1816. They were responsible for supervising the shoeing of the horses, carried out by farriers. Brigade chaplains followed the unit on all campaigns. ...

A characteristic speciality of the English officers was the mess, which was unknown in Hannover, and Colonel v. Langwerth wrote in 1803, "We are eating together in what is called the mess and this is more important to the English than their duties."

The mess served as a social gathering point, made life cheaper and inspired good comradeship. The problem of seniority was solved by electing a president and a vice-president every week. Everybody except field officers and the younger officers (with less than two years of duty) could be elected. The president served the soup and kept order during the meal. In toasting, it was the law to empty the glass. "Fill what you will, but drink what you fill." Conversation was not as formal as on duty. Life in the mess was important to teach the officers to become real gentlemen.

The Germans' love of music soon led to popularity of the Legion in England. The cavalry had brass music, the infantry in addition had woodwinds. Some so-called "janissaries" (mostly coloured people from the West Indies who wore gaudy clothes, comprising of green jackets with red sleeves and a turban on their heads) played the bass drum, cymbals, triangle, and a snare drum mounted on mules during marches. In the beginning, the hussar regiments had janissaries also, but soon abandoned them. A "Jingling Johnny"★ and fifers completed the marching music of the infantry. Every unit had its own march.

After: Bernhard Schwertfeger, Geschichte, der Koniglich Deitschen Legion 1803−1816, Erster Band, Hannover and Leipzig 1907, pages 41−46.

Janissary
Of the 1st line battalion K.G.L.

Used as bandsmen in a number of regiments. Usually, Christian boys converted to Islam by the Turks, then captured or escaped to European armies.

★ Jingling Johnny – a stick with bells – a glockenspiel (percussion instrument of metal bars which are struck with hammer; a sort of xylophone).

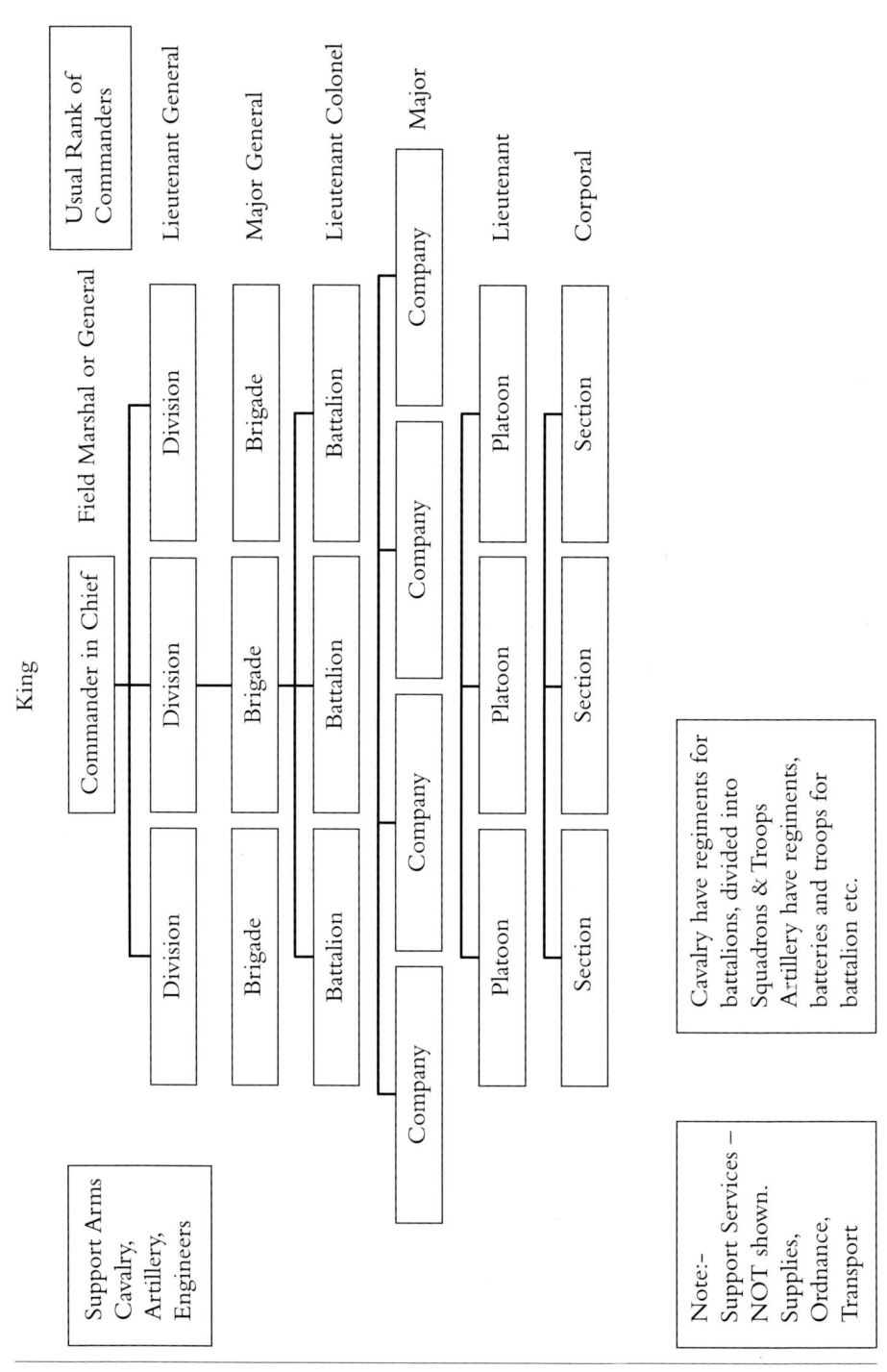

King

Usual Rank of Commanders

Field Marshal or General	
Commander in Chief	
Division	Lieutenant General
Brigade	Major General
Battalion	Lieutenant Colonel
Company	Major
Platoon	Lieutenant
Section	Corporal

Support Arms
Cavalry,
Artillery,
Engineers

Cavalry have regiments for battalions, divided into Squadrons & Troops
Artillery have regiments, batteries and troops for battalion etc.

Note:-
Support Services –
NOT shown.
Supplies,
Ordnance,
Transport

ORDER OF BATTLE (ORBAT) WATERLOO

Anglo – Allied Army

I Corps – The Prince of Orange – 32,589

1st British Division – Major General G. Cooke – 4,671

1st British (Guards) Brigade – Major General P. Maitland – 1,997

2nd Battalion of the 1st Foot Guards Regiment – Major H. Askew – 976
3rd Battalion of the 1st Foot Guards Regiment – Major Wm Stewart – 1,021

2nd British (Guards) Brigade – Major General J. Byng

2nd Battalion of 2nd (Coldstream) Foot Guards – Major A.G. Woodford – 1,003
2nd Battalion of 3rd (Scots) Foot Guards – Major F. Hepburn – 1,061

Artillery – Lt Col Adye

Capt. Ch. F. Sandham's Battery, RFA – 9 pounders – 390
Major Kuhlmann's Battery, KGLHA – 220

3rd British Division – Lt General Charles Alten – 6,970

5th British Brigade – Major General C. Halkett

2nd Battalion of the 30th (Cambridgeshire) Regiment – Major W. Bailey – 615
2nd Battalion of the 33rd (1st Yorkshire West Riding) Regiment –
Lt Col W.K. Elphinstone – 561
2nd Battalion of the 69th (South Lincolnshire) Regiment – Lt Col C. Morice – 516
2nd Battalion of the 73rd (Highland) Regiment – Lt Col W.G. Harris – 562

2nd King's German Legion Brigade – Colonel von Ompteda

1st (Rifles) Light Infantry Battalion – Lt Col L. Bussche – 423
2nd (Rifles) Light Infantry Battalion – Major G. Baring – 337
5th Line Infantry Battalion – Lt-Col W.B. Linsingen – 379
8th Line Infantry Battalion – Major Schroeder – 388

1st Hanoverian Brigade – Major General Kielmansegge

Bremen Field Battalion – Lt Col Langrehr – 512
Verden Field Battalion – Major de Senkopp – 533
Duke of York 1st Field Battalion – Major von Bülow – 607
Lüneburg Light Battalion – Lt Col von Klencke – 595
Grubenhagen Light Battalion – Lt Col von Wurmberg – 621
Field-Jäger Battalion – 321

Artillery – Lt Col J.S. Williamson

Major Lloyd's battery, RFA – 9 pounders – 390
Captain A. Cleve's Battery, KGLFA – 86

2nd Netherlands Division – Lt. General H.G. de Perponcher-Slednitzky – 8,177

1st Brigade – Major General W.F. van Bijlandt – 3,452

7th Belgian Line Infantry Regiment – Lt Col F.C. Vandensande – 701
27th Dutch Jägers – Lt Col J.W. Grunebosch – 809
5th Dutch Militia Battalion – Lt Col J.J. Westenberg – 482
7th Dutch Militia Battalion – Colonel H. Singendonck – 675
8th Dutch Militia Battalion – Colonel W.A. de Jongh – 566

2nd Brigade – Prince Bernhard of Saxe-Weimar – 4,725

1st Battalion of the 2nd Nassau Regiment – Major F. Sattler – 925
2nd Battalion of the 2nd Nassau Regiment – Major P. von Normann – 885
3rd Battalion of the 2nd Nassau Regiment – Major G. Hegmann – 899
1st Battalion of the Orange-Nassau Regiment No. 28 – Lt Col W.F. von Dressel – 893
2nd Battalion of the Orange-Nassau Regiment No. 28 – Major P. Schleijer – 688
1 Company Nassau Volunteer Jägers – Captain E. Bergmann – 177

Artillery – Major C. van Opstall

Captain A. Bijleveld's Dutch Battery, HA – 107
Captain E.J. Stievenart's Belgian Battery, FA – 6 pounders – 119

3rd Netherlands Division – Lt. General D.H. Chassé – 7,146

1st Brigade – Colonel H. Detmers – 3,298

6th Dutch Militia Battalion – Lt Col A. van Thielen – 492
17th Dutch Militia Battalion – Lt Col N. van Molz Wieling – 534
19th Dutch Militia Battalion – Major H. Boellaerdt – 467
2nd Brigade – Major General A.K.J.G. d'Aubremé – 3,848
3rd Belgian Line Infantry Regiment – Lt Col E.P. l'Honneux – 629
12th Dutch Line Infantry Regiment – Colonel D.O. Bagelaar – 431
13th Dutch Line Infantry Regiment – Lt Col F.N.L. Aberson – 664
36th Belgian Jager – Lt Col Ch. Goethals – 633
3rd Dutch Militia Battalion – Lt Col F.E. van Lawick van Pabst – 592
10th Dutch Militia Battalion – Lt Col G.F. Brade – 632

Artillery – Major J.L.D. van der Smissen

Captain C.F. Krahmer de Bichin's Belgian Battery, HA, 6 pounders – 123
Captain J.H. Lux's Dutch battery, FA, 6 pounders – 121

II Corps – Lt General R. Hill – 25,911

2nd British Division – Lt General H. Clinton – 7,443

3rd British Brigade – Major General F. Adam

1st Btn of the 52nd (Oxfordshire) Light Infantry – Lt Col J. Colborne – 1,038
1st Btn of the 71st (Glasgow Highland) Light Infantry – Lt Col J. Reynell – 810
6 Companies of the 2nd Btn of the 95th Rifles Regiment – Major A.G. Norcott – 585
2 Companies of the 3rd Btn of the 95th Rifles Regiment – Major J. Ross – 188

1st King's German Legion Brigade – Colonel C.L.A. du Plat

1st Line Battalion – Major W. Robertson – 411
2nd Line Battalion – Major G. Muller – 437
3rd Line Battalion – Lt Col F. de Wissell – 494
4th Line Battalion – Major F. Reb – 416

3rd Hanoverian Brigade – Colonel Hugh Halkett

Bremervörde Landwehr Battalion – Lt Col Schulenberg – 632
Duke of York's 2nd Battalion – Major Munster – 612
Duke of York's 3rd Battalion – Major Hunefeld – 588
Salzgitter Landwehr Battalion – Major Hammerstein – 622

Artillery – Lt Col C. Gold

Captain Bolton's Battery, RFA, (4) 9-lbers, (2) howitzers – 390
Major A. Sympher's Battery, KGLHA – 220

4th British Division – Lt General Charles Colville – 7,704

4th British Brigade – Colonel H.H. Mitchell

3rd Btn of 14th (Buckinghamshire) Regiment – Major F.C. Tidy – 571
1st Btn of 23rd (Royal Welsh) Fusiliers – Lt Col H.W. Ellis – 647
51st (2nd Yorkshire West Riding) Light Infantry – Lt Col H. Mitchell – 549

6th British Brigade – Major General G. Johnstone

2nd Btn of 35th (Sussex) Regiment – Major C. McAlister – 570
1st Btn of 54th (West Norfolk) Regiment – Lt Col J. Waldegrave – 541
2nd Btn of 59th (South Lincolnshire) Regiment – Lt Col H. Austin – 461
1st Btn of 91st (Argyllshire) Regiment – Lt Col W. Douglas - 824

6th Hanoverian Brigade – Major General J. Lyon

Lauenberg Field Battalion – Lt Col Benort – 553
Calenberg Field Battalion – 634
Nieuberg Landwehr Battalion – 629
Hoya Landwehr Battalion – Lt Col Grote – 625
Bentheim Landwehr Battalion – Major Croupp – 608

Artillery – Lt Col J. Hawker

Major J. Brome's Battery, RFA – 260
Captain von Rettberg's Battery, Hanoverian Foot Artillery – 232

1st Netherlands Division – Lt General J.A. Stedman – 6,662

1st Brigade – Major General F. d'Hauw – 3,269

4th Belgian Line Infantry Regiment – Lt Col E. de Man – 548
6th Dutch Line Infantry Regiment – Lt Col P.A. Twent – 431
16th Dutch Jägers – Lt Col S.R. van Hulstein – 490
9th Dutch Militia Battalion – Lt Col J.J. Simons – 565
14th Dutch Militia Battalion – Lt Col W. Poolman – 586
15th Dutch Militia Battalion – Lt Col P.C. Colthoff – 659

2nd Brigade – Major General D.J. de Eerens – 3,393

1st Belgian Line Infantry Regiment – Lt Col W. Kuijck – 682
18th Dutch Jägers – Lt Col van Aremberg – 798
1st Dutch Militia Battalion – Lt Col F.A. Guicherit – 591
2nd Dutch Militia Battalion – Lt Col A.W. Senn van Bazel – 582
18th Dutch Militia Battalion – Lt Col F.W. van Ommeren – 515

Artillery

Captain P. Wijnand's Foot Battery, 6 pounders – 119

Netherlands Indian Brigade – Lt General C.H.W. Anthing – 3,729

1st Battalion of the 5th Dutch (East Indies) Infantry Regiment – Lt Col B. Bischoff
2nd Battalion of the 5th Dutch (East Indies) Infantry Regiment – Lt Col F. Stoecker
Both battalions total: 1,541
Flank Companies of the 19th and 20th Line Infantry Regiment – Col W. Schenck – 536
10th Dutch (West Indies) Jägers – Col H.W. Rancke – 704
11th Dutch (West Indies) Jägers – Lt Col F. Knotzer – 718
Captain C.J. Riesz's Battery, FA, 6 pounders – 120

Reserve – Wellington – 51,686

5th Division – Lt General T. Picton – 7,651

8th British Brigade – Major General J. Kempt

1st Btn of 28th (North Gloucestershire) Regiment – Lt Col C.P. Belson – 557
1st Btn of 32nd (Cornwall) Regiment – Major J. Hicks – 662
1st Btn of 79th (Cameron) Highlanders – Lt Col N. Douglas – 703
6 Companies of the 1st Btn of 95th Rifles – Lt Col A.F. Barnard – 549

9th British Brigade – Major General D. Pack

3rd Btn of 1st (Royal Scots) Regiment – Major C. Campbell – 604
1st Btn of 42nd (Royal Highland) Regiment – Lt Col R. Macarx – 526
2nd Btn of 44th (East Sussex) Regiment – Lt Col J.M. Hammerton – 455
1st Btn of 92nd (Gordon) Highlanders – Lt Col J. Cameron – 558

5th Hanoverian Brigade – Colonel von Vincke

Hamen Landwehr Battalion – Lt Col Klencke – 669
Giffhorn Landwehr Battalion – Major Hammerstein – 617
Peine Landwehr Battalion – Major Westphalen – 611
Hildesheim Landwehr Battalion – Major Rheden – 617

Artillery – Major A. Heisse

Major F. Rogers' Battery, RFA – 260
Captain Braun's Battery, Hanoverian FA – 233

6th Division – Lt General L. Cole – 5,799

10th British Brigade – Major General J. Lambert

1st Btn of 4th (King's Own) Regiment – Lt Col F. Brooke – 669
1st Btn of 27th (Inniskilling) Regiment – Captain J. Hare – 698
1st Btn of 40th (2nd Somersetshire) Regiment – Major A. Heyland – 761
2nd Btn of 81st (Loyals) Infantry Regiment – 439

4th Hanoverian Brigade – Colonel Best

Lüneburg Landwehr Battalion – Lt Col Ramdohr – 624
Verden Landwehr Battalion – Major Decken – 621
Osterode Landwehr Battalion – Major Reden – 677
Münden Landwehr Battalion – Major de Smidt – 660

Artillery – Lt Col Brückmann

Major G.W. Unett's Battery, RFA – 260
Captain J. Sinclair's Battery, RFA – 390

British Reserve Artillery – Major P. Drummond – 1,260

Lt Colonel H.D. Ross's Battery, RHA, (5) 9-lbers, (1) heavy 5.5" howitzer – 175
Major G. Beane's Battery, RHA, (5) 9-lbers, (1) heavy 5.5" howitzer – 175
Major Morrisson's Battery, RFA, (4) 18 pounder – 260
Captain T. Hutchesson's Battery, RFA (4) 18 pounder – 260
Captain Ilbert's Battery, RFA, (6) 18 pounder – 390

7th Division – 3,233 (including garrison)

7th British Brigade

2nd Btn of 25th (K.O.S.B.) Regiment – 388
2nd Btn of 37th (Hampshire) Regiment – 491
2nd Btn of 78th (Seaforth Highlanders) Regiment – 337
1st Foreign Battalion – Lt Col Belleville – 595

British Garrison Troops

13th Veterans Battalion – 683
2nd Garrison Battalion – 739

The Brunswick Corps (Black Legion) – Duke of Brunswick – 6,808

Avant Garde Battalion (including 2 coys of Oels Jägers and 2 coys Light Infantry – Major von Ranschenplatt – 672
Hussar Regiment – 69
Uhlan Squadron – 232

1st (Light) Brigade – Major General Olfermans

Guard Battalion – 672
1st Light Infantry Battalion – 672
2nd Light Infantry Battalion – 672
3rd Light Infantry Battalion – 672

2nd (Line) Brigade – Lt Col von Buttler

1st Line Battalion – 672
2nd Line Battalion – 672
3rd Line Battalion - 672

Artillery – Major von Lubeck

Captain von Heinemann's Battery, HA (8) – 216
Major von Moll's Battery, FA (8) – 294

Hanoverian Reserve Corps – Lt General F. von der Decken – 9,312

1st Brigade – Lt Col von Bennigsen

Hoya Field Battalion
Mölln Landwehr Battalion
Bremerlehe Landwehr Battalion

2nd Brigade – Colonel von Beaulieu

Nordheim Landwehr Battalion
Ahlefeldt Landwehr Battalion
Springe Landwehr Battalion

3rd Brigade – Lt Col von Bodecken

Altendorff Landwehr Battalion
Celle Landwehr Battalion
Ratzeburg Landwehr Battalion

4th Brigade – Lt Col von Wissel

Hannover Landwehr Battalion
Uelzen Landwehr Battalion
Neustadt Landwehr Battalion
Diepholz Landwehr Battalion

Nassau Contingent – Major General A.H.E. von Kruse – 2,900

1st Battalion of the 1st (Duke of Nassau) Infantry Regiment – Major von Weijhers – 951
2nd Battalion of the 1st (Duke of Nassau) Infantry Regiment – Major von Nauendorf – 943
Landwehr Battalion of the 1st (Duke of Nassau) Infantry Regiment – Major von Preen - 947

Cavalry – Lt General Uxbridge – 11,205

1st British (Household Cavalry) Brigade – Major General E. Somerset

2 sq of the 1st Life Guards – Lt Col S. Ferrior – 228
2 sq of the 2nd Life Guards – Lt Col E.P. Lygon – 231
2 sq of the Royal Horse (Blues) Guards – Lt Col R. Chambre Hill – 237
4 sq of the 1st (King's) Dragoon Guards – Lt Col Wm. Fuller – 530

2nd British (Union) Brigade – Major General Wm. Ponsonby

3 sq of the 1st (Royal) Dragoons – Lt Col A.B. Clifton – 394
3 sq of the 2nd (Royal Scots Greys) Dragoons – Lt Col J.I. Hamilton – 391
3 sq of the 6th (Inniskilling) Dragoons – Lt Col J. Muter – 396

3rd British (Light) Brigade – Major General W. Dörnberg

3 sq of the 23rd Light Dragoons – Lt Col J. Earl of Portarlington – 387
4 sq of the 1st Light Dragoons, KGL – Lt Col J. Bülow – 462
4 sq of the 2nd Light Dragoons, KGL – Lt Col C. de Jonquieres – 419

4th British Brigade – Major General J. Vandeleur

3 sq of the 11th Light Dragoons – Lt Col J.W. Sleigh – 390
3 sq of the 12th (Prince of Wales') Light Dragoons – Lt Col F.C. Ponsonby – 388
3 sq of the 16th (Queen's) Light Dragoons – Lt Col J. Hay – 393

5th British (Hussar) Brigade – Major General C. Grant

3 sq of the 7th (Queen's Own) Hussars – Lt Col E. Kerrison – 380
3 sq of the 15th (King's) Hussars – Lt Col E. Dalrymple – 392
4 sq of the 2nd Hussars, KGL – Lt Col Linsingen – 564

6th British Brigade – Major General H. Vivian

3 sq of the 10th (Prince of Wales' Own Royal) Hussars – Lt Col G. Quentin – 390
3 sq of the 18th Hussars – Lt Col H. Murray – 396
4 sq of the 1st Hussars, KGL – Lt Col A. Wissell – 493

7th British Brigade – Colonel F. von Arentsschildt

3 sq of the 13th Light Dragoons – Lt Col P. Doherty – 390
4 sq of the 3rd Hussars, KGL – Lt Col Meijer – 622

British Horse Artillery (Attached to Cavalry) – Lt Col A. Macdonald – 1,050

Lt Colonel R. Gardiner's Battery, RHA, (5) light 6-pounders, (1) light 5.5" howitzer – 175
Lt Colonel J. Webber Smyth's Battery, RHA, (5) light 6-pounders, (1) 5.5" howitzer - 175
Major R. Bull's Battery, RHA, (96) heavy 5.5" howitzers – 175

Captain E.C. Whinyates' Battery, Mounted Rocket Corps, RHA, (5) light 6-pounders

(13) sections, each comprising (8) 6-pound rockets – 175
2nd Captain Alexander Cavalié Mercer's Battery, RHA – 193
Lieutenant Hincks, (2) 9-pounders
Lieutenant Leathes, (1) 9-pounder, (1) heavy 5.5" howitzer
Lieutenant Breton, (2) 9-pounders
Captain Wm. N. Ramsay's Battery, RHA, 9 pounder – 175

1st Hanoverian Brigade – Colonel H.S.G.F. von Estorff

4 sq of the Prince Regent's Hussars – Lt Col Kielmansegge – 596
4 sq of the Bremen & Verden Hussars – Colonel Bussche – 589
4 sq of the Duke of Cumberland's Hussars – 497

Netherlands Cavalry Division – Lt General J.A. de Collaert

Heavy Cavalry Brigade – Major General A.D. Trip van Zoudtlant – 1,237

3 sq of the 1st (Dutch) Carabiniers – Lt Col L.P. Coenegracht – 446
3 sq of the 2nd (Belgian) Carabiniers – Colonel J.B. de Bruijn – 399
3 sq of the 3rd (Dutch) Carabiniers – Lt Col C.M. Lechleitner – 392

1st Light Brigade – Major General C.E. de Ghigny – 1,086

4 sq of the 4th (Dutch) Light Dragoons – Lt Col J.C. Renno – 647
3 sq of the 8th (Belgian) Hussars – Lt Col I.L. Duvivier – 439

2nd Light Brigade – Major General J.B. van Merlen – 1,082

3 sq of the 5th (Belgian) Light Dragoons – Lt Col E.A.J.G. Mercx – 441
4 sq of the 6th (Dutch) Hussars – Lt Col W.F. Boreel – 641

Horse Artillery

Captain A. Petter's Half-Battery, 6 pounder – 132
Captain A.R.W. Gey van Pittius' Half-Battery, 6 pounder – 109

Also:

Corps of Royal Engineers – 41
Corps of Royal Sappers and Miners – 800
Royal Wagon Train
Royal Staff Corps

Notes on infantry:

British Infantry Regiment = 2 Battalions (except 1st, 14th, 27th, 60th, and 95th Regiments)
1 British Infantry Battalion = 10 Companies (8 centre and 2 flank)
95th British Rifles Regiment = 3 Battalions
1 Battalion = 10 Companies of 113 men each
1 Company = 2 Platoons
1 Platoon = 2 Squads
1 Netherlands Infantry Regiment = 1 Battalion = 8 Companies (6 centre and 2 flank)

Artillery
All Royal Foot Artillery had 9-pounders at Waterloo
All Royal Horse Artillery Batteries had 193 men, 226 horses, and comprised (except as noted)
Left Division = (2) 9-pounders
Centre Division = (1) 9-pounder and 1 heavy 5.5" howitzer
Right Division = (2) 9-pounders

Further Reading

Books in Bexhill Library

The King's German Legion (1) 1803–1812
By Mike Chappell *(Osprey Men-at-Arms Series)*

The King's German Legion (2) 1812–1816
By Mike Chappell *(Osprey Men-at-Arms Series)*

Wellington's Infantry (2)
By Bryan Fosten *(Osprey Men-at-Arms Series)*

The Hanoverian Army of the Napoleonic Wars
By Peter Hofschroer & Bryan Fosten *(Osprey Men-at-Arms Series)*

British Cavalryman 1792–1815
By Philip Haythornthwaite & Richard Hook *(Osprey Warrior Series)*

The Eagle's Last Triumph – Napoleon's Victory at Ligny, June 1815
By Andrew Uffindell

On the Fields of Glory – The Battlefields of the 1815 Campaign
By Andrew Uffindell and Michael Corum

Hougoumont – The Key to Victory at Waterloo
By Julian Paget and Derek Saunders

Memoirs of Baron Ompteda: ★ Colonel in the King's German Legion during the Napoleonic Wars.

The Wheatley Diary: ★ A Journal and Sketchbook kept during the Peninsular War and Waterloo Campaign
Edited by Christopher Hibbert

History of the King's German Legion ★ Volume 1.
By N. Ludlow Beamish F.R.S.

History of the King's German Legion ★ Volume 11.
By N. Ludlow Beamish F.R.S.

There is also a file containing the complete list of **The Waterloo Roll Call of the K.G.L.** ★

★ These four books, and file of King's German Legion Waterloo Roll Call, are in the reference section of Bexhill library.

Some Websites to Contact Regarding The King's German Legion

1. King's German Legion (UK)
www.kingsgermanlegion.org.uk

2. King's German Legion
@online www.kgl.de

3. The King's German Legion (UK)
@onlinewww.regiments.org

4. The Melancholy Hussar of the German Legion 1889, 1912
gaslight.mtroyal.ab.ca

5. Osprey Publishing/The King's German Legion (1)
www.ospreypublishing.com

6. The Organization of the King's German Artillery 1814–1815
www.napoleonseries.org

7. **Lebendiges Museum – Termine**
www.lebendiges-museum.de

8. **Armies in Plastic, Inc. – Home Page**
www.armiesinplastic.com

9. **British Infantry Regiments at Waterloo – King's German Legion**
www.warflag.com

10. **La Haye Saint, King's German Legion**
www.war-art.com

11. **Alphabetical Listing of Network Sites**
network.historychannel.com

12. **History of the King's German Legion N Ludlow Beamish**
www.reference-book.co.uk/N–Ludlow–Beamish-History-of-the-King's-Ger-1897632126.html

13. **AGFHS – Len Metzner's Indexes**
www.art-science.com

14. **King's German Legion Light Dragoons**
www.canada-shops.com

15. **King's German Legion Light Infantry**
www.armouryshop.co.uk

16. **Napoleonic Memoirs: O's**
napoleonic-literature.com

Acknowledgements

Back Cover – Re-enactment Group – Courtesy **Bexhill Observer**

Page(s)
8 & 9   Uniforms: K.G.L. Soldiers – Vol. 1 History of the KGL by N. Ludlow Beamish. Permission of **The Naval & Military Press Ltd.**

11 and front cover   Christian von Ompteda Courtesy of **Mr Bryan Fosten**

36   St Peter's Church, Births, Deaths & Marriages – Permission of **Janet Harris**

51   Plaque at La Haye Sainte – Courtesy **Bexhill Observer**

57   Waterloo – 11.30am, 18th June –
59   Waterloo - Repulse of Imperial Guard From book **"On the Fields of Glory"**: Permission of **Andrew Uffindell** and **Greenhill Books**

61   Command and Staff Permission of **Michael A. Taenzer**

Page
78   Conrad Olderhausen courtesy of **Hastings Museum and Art Gallery**

Thanks are due to **Mr Julian Porter**, Curator of **Bexhill Museum** for permission to use the following illustrations:-

2   Coat of Arms of Hanover
11   The Duke of Cambridge
12   Old Bexhill Barracks in Lower Belle Hill area
14   Part of Bexhill Manor Map showing barracks of K.G.L.
16   Bexhill Village 1794
19   Major Baring
22   The Duke of Wellington
23   Lt-General Charles von Alten
24   Colin Halkett
25   Edmund Wheatley & Illustration of first Exhibition of K.G.L. in Bexhill Museum
26   A drawing of a K.G.L. soldier by a 9-year-old boy when visiting Bexhill Museum
27   Framed portrait of Christian Frederick William Baron Ompteda

Old Soldiers Tell Tales ...
News of the Past

In 1992, from the archives of Hastings Museum and Art Gallery, a picture emerged of Conrad Olderhausen who was in the King's German Legion. It was all thanks to the researches of Bexhill Hanoverian Study Group and the Museum that Conrad Olderhausen's story came to light.

The portrait was drawn by artist Ella Taylor and presented to Hastings Museum and Art Gallery by her. It shows Conrad Olderhausen at the age of 84, proudly wearing his Military General Service Medal and his Waterloo Medal. Five clasps were awarded for service at Albuhera, the Pyrenees, Vittoria, St Sebastian and Nivelle.

Born in Hameln 1779, Conrad served in the 1st Light Battalion of the King's German Legion in barracks at Bexhill waiting to cross the Channel to join in the conflict against Napoleon. At the Battle of Waterloo, at the age of 35/36, he was a bugler. After Waterloo, Conrad served three years in the 85th Regiment as a musician and then five years in the Hereford Militia under the Marquis of Salisbury. Afterwards he is believed to have served aboard HMS Minerva in India and China and, finally, for three years aboard HMS Hyperion.

However, recent research by the Bexhill Hanoverian Study Group, has brought to light some additional facts regarding Conrad:-

Conrad Olderhausen and Mercy, his wife, are listed as being in Portugal on 25th March 1813, but have no children. Mercy Olderhausen died in 1835 at the age of 51 appearing on the burial register of St Peter's Church, Bexhill. ... In January 1836 Conrad married Ann Parkes at Ninfield. Their daughter Mercy was born and baptised in June of the same year. Their son John was born in 1838.

Conrad was a well-known figure in his day; he was a member of Hastings Old Town Band and, later on, sold refreshments at Fairlight Glen. Conrad died at his home in Ore, Hastings 11th August 1869, aged 89 years. He was buried at St Helen's Church, Ore.

Subscribers List

1. Mr Dave Allan

2. Herr Georg Baumann

3 Mr Paul Beckwith

4. Bexhill Old Town Preservation Society

5. The Reverend James Bogle

6. Dr Peter Boyden

7. Mr Eric Brown

8. Mr & Mr Stanley Bullock

9. Mr Paul Chamberlain

10. Mr & Mrs Raymond Child

11. Mr A.J. Clements

12. Mr Peter Cole

13. Mr Raymond P. Cusick

14. Msr Guy Delvaux

15. Mrs Kate Eagers

16. Mr Tony Faulkner

17. Major (Ret'd) R.J.D. Gardner

18. Mrs Lillian Glenn

19. Mrs Carol Godfrey

20. Ms Janet Harris

21. Mrs Jane Jones

22. Mr & Mrs Michael Kent

23. Mr David Lawrence

24. Mrs Jean Lea

25. Mr Ian Lightbown

26. Mrs Jean Malkin

27. Mr Fred Rye

28. Mr Brian Scott

29. Ms Dee Stanley

30. Mr Eric Tomkins

31. Mr Andrew Whiteley

32. Mr Dennis Wraight

In Bexhill, there is a Study Group which meets every third Wednesday of the month at 7.30 pm in the Northern Hotel, Sea Road, Bexhill.

The prime function of the Study Group is to research the King's German Legion.

The Bexhill Hanoverian Study Group, together with the Old Town Preservation Society, erected a plaque in the Memorial Gardens, Barrack Road, Bexhill, dedicated to the personnel of the King's German Legion who are buried there.

The Study Group has also been instrumental in placing a plaque on the wall of La Haye Sainte, Waterloo, where the King's German Legion fought a bitter battle on 18th June 1815.

Why not join the Bexhill Hanoverian Study Group and learn about the K.G.L. troops in Bexhill during the Napoleonic period and various battles in which the K.G.L. took part?

For further details, please contact: Stella Child, 83 Turkey Road, Bexhill-on-Sea, East Sussex TN39 5HH. Tel. No. 01424 212130.

Back cover picture: K.G.L. Light bn – Re-enactment group on Barrack site – Bexhill